BEHIND
THE WIRE

BEHIND THE WIRE

EVERYDAY LIFE AS A POW

Tom Guttridge

AMBERLEY

First published 2017

Amberley Publishing
The Hill, Stroud
Gloucestershire, GL5 4EP

www.amberley-books.com

British Library Cataloguing in Publication Data.
A catalogue record for this book is available from the British Library.

ISBN 978 1 4456 7310 3 (print)
ISBN 978 1 4456 7311 0 (ebook)

Origination by Amberley Publishing.
Printed in Great Britain.

CONTENTS

FOREWORD

'Calais burned. From the Citadel to the Courgain every street was on fire. A giant, choking cloud of smoke drifted over the harbour, so that only the spire of Notre Dame and the clock tower of the Hotel de Ville could be seen from the shore.'

This was the scene – as described by Airey Neave in *The Flames of Calais* – as the northern French port fell into German hands on 26 May 1940 following four days of intense fighting. The battle was a pivotal event in the first year of the Second World War, for although Calais eventually fell, the 3,000 British, 800 French, and a lesser number of Belgian troops had succeeded in holding up the German advance long enough to facilitate the evacuation of 338,000 of their compatriots from Dunkirk 30 miles away. In a comment written after the war, Prime Minister Sir Winston Churchill wrote, 'Calais was the crux. Many other causes might have prevented the deliverance of Dunkirk, but it is certain the three days gained by the defence of Calais enabled the Gravelines Waterline to be held, and that without this … all would have been cut off and lost.'

For the survivors of Calais, it was also a pivotal event on an individual level. Only around sixty British troops escaped, mostly in boats across the Channel. Others were killed or seriously wounded, but for the vast majority the fall of Calais was the beginning of a different kind of battle – a seemingly endless struggle for survival in prisoner-of-war camps in Germany and Poland. Among them was Corporal Tom Guttridge of the First Battalion the Rifle Brigade (he appears in some records as Lance Corporal – a demotion that I believe resulted from one of the pranks for which he was known). Tom – my father – had already completed a seven-year stint as a regular soldier; but that was in peacetime. As with most of those around him, Calais was his first experience of shots fired in anger, and was also to be his last. Unlike Airey Neave, who went on to achieve fame as the first British officer to escape successfully from

Colditz (and, tragically, as the victim of a terrorist car bomb at the House of Commons in 1979), Tom spent the next five years in captivity, unaware if and when he would see his homeland and family again.

When he did finally return in May 1945, he brought with him not only memories of many unforgettable experiences but a collection of photographs of the Calais battlefield, the PoW camps and Malta during the five years he spent there with the Rifle Brigade before the war. The Calais pictures were taken by a German soldier after the battle ended and I believe that most of the PoW shots were obtained from camp guards in exchange for cigarettes that arrived in Red Cross parcels and became a form of currency.

As a child growing up in the 1950s and 1960s, I was fascinated by Dad's stories about the fighting at Calais and his years in Stalag VIII B and Stalag 383. But it was not until the 1990s that I suggested that he write everything down. As well as describing his Calais and PoW experiences in vivid detail, he also wrote about his seven years in the Rifle Brigade in the 1930s. My father died in 2004 and it fell to me to prepare this book for publication. In doing so I considered omitting his peacetime memories on the grounds that they did not directly relate to his PoW years. Having reread them, however, I decided to retain them for two reasons: firstly because they provide a rare and fascinating insight into life as a regular soldier in the 1930s; secondly because to some extent they prepared him for the wartime challenges to follow and therefore are relevant. I have also added a postscript summarising my father's post-war life and describing the startling moment in 2013 that provided a new impetus for publication. I have also added a number of pictures from other sources to fill illustrative gaps in various parts of the story.

Roger Guttridge,
June 2017

CHAPTER 1

JOINING UP, PASSING OUT

I was eighteen and fed up with the daily grind of travelling to work in London's Hatton Garden. For some time I had been turning over in my mind the possibility of perhaps joining one of the services. On 5 April 1932, I finally made up my mind, and instead of heading for the office, I set off for Whitehall. I entered the recruiting office of the War Department and applied to join the Guards. Being only 5 foot 8½ inches tall, I was told by the Guards' recruiting sergeant to go away and put on another 2½ inches. In other words, to get lost!

However, the officer recruiting for the Rifle Brigade welcomed me with open arms. I successfully passed the medical and intelligence tests, and two hours after entering the building I found myself a member of one of the crack regiments of the British Army. I received my two weeks' pay (the handsome sum of £1) and was instructed to return home and await instructions on when to report to the Rifle Brigade depot at Peninsula Barracks, Winchester. I always remember the date I joined up because the Derby winner that year was April the Fifth. You can imagine the consternation of my parents when I broke the news to them. Ten days later my railway travelling warrant and final instructions dropped through the letter box, and two days after that I was on my way to Winchester.

A number of young lads alighted from the train at Winchester station and it was obvious that we were all there for the same purpose. At the station entrance we were met by two army sergeants – one from the Rifle Brigade and the other from the sister regiment, the King's Royal Rifle Corps. Those men for the Rifle Brigade were allotted to one 3-ton army lorry; the group for the KRRC boarded another 3-tonner. The two regiments shared the same barrack complex, the Rifle Brigade occupying one side of the huge drill square, the KRRC the other. There was great rivalry between the two regiments and little love lost between the two camps, who tried to outdo each other in smartness, general efficiency, sport and all other aspects of army life.

Serial No. *1/R.B/23h.*   Army Form B.108.

Regular Army.

Certificate of Service.

Army No. *6912697.*

Surname   *GUTTRIDGE.*

Christian Names   *Thomas Reginald*

Enlisted at   *London*

Enlisted on   *25·4·1932.*

Corps for which enlisted

The Rifle Brigade

NOTE.—Attention is specially directed to Pages 2, 6 & 7.

The opening page of Tom's Rifle Brigade record of service recording his enlistment in 1932.

The Gatehouse at Winchester Barracks *c.* 1955. (Photo: Oxfordshire County Council – Oxfordshire History Centre; Hampshire Record Office, ref: 170A12W/P/8040)

It was a strange feeling going through the massive barrack gates for the first time, and although we did not know it then, we were not to see the outside world again for another four weeks. It soon became clear to me that the honeymoon period was over, and I began to have doubts as to whether I had done the right thing by joining up. As far as I can remember, we began with a march down to the Quartermaster's stores to be kitted out with uniform, etc. I remember that my greatcoat nearly touched the ground. I was told that I would grow sufficiently in the next nine months for it to fit me perfectly. After this we headed for the barber's shop. In those days a haircut consisted of the clippers going straight up the back of the head and then round the sides, leaving as little as possible on top. The barber had a huge stomach, which he pressed against you. A wet cigarette dangling from the corner of his mouth was apparently a permanent feature. He was known to all as Sweeney Todd after the villain of Victorian fiction who despatched his victims by pulling a lever on his barber's chair and tipping them through a trapdoor. I was not despatched by our Sweeney Todd but I felt very cold around the head when he had finished.

Our living quarters consisted of dormitories with accommodation for twelve soldiers and an adjoining washroom and shower. There were six beds on either side of the room, each with a locker above, and a bedside cabinet. The bedding consisted of three coir-filled biscuits (coconut matting squares), two calico sheets, two blankets, and a rather hard bolster. Until you got used to it, it was like laying your head on a concrete block.

Reveille was sounded by a bugler at 6.30 a.m. You had thirty minutes to wash, dress and be ready for the first parade of the morning. This consisted of half-an-hour of loosening up exercises in the gym. After a short rest period, it was then down to the dining hall for breakfast. The food served out at the Rifle depot for 'other ranks' can only be described as awful. Unlike county regiments, the Green Jackets, as the two regiments were jointly known, did not receive a catering grant from a county council. All the food and drink supplied to other ranks was funded by officers of the two regiments. Breakfast usually consisted of one thin rasher of bacon and a ladle of baked beans. This culinary delight was known as 'chinstrap and birdseed'. Twice a week we would have a change and be served with chunks of boiled liver in gravy. This dish was pretty obnoxious.

Part of the main drill square was covered with gravel, and on one occasion a sack of peas split open while being transported to the cookhouse. To our surprise, the peas plus gravel were hastily shovelled back into the sack and conveyed to their destination. Dinner that day consisted of stewed mutton, peas, and potatoes. When the peas were ladled onto the plates you could hear

The gravelled drill square and Barracks in Tom's time. (Photo: Hampshire Record Office: The Royal Green Jackets Archive: 170A12W/P/4248)

a distinct tinkling sound. The orderly officer then came round to each table, as was the practice, and asked if there were any complaints. I stood up and said, 'I have some peas in my gravel, sir,' for which remark I was put on a charge and ordered to be outside the Company Commander's office at 9 a.m. next day. When the hour arrived, it was 'Hat off, right turn, quick march' into the office. I was duly admonished and awarded seven days' fatigues.

Fatigues had to be carried out in your own leisure time, after all the daily parades were completed. One of my tasks was to empty the coal shed, scrub the floor, whitewash the walls, and put all the coal back. Another job was to scrub out the white chalk lines that had been marked out on the parade ground in readiness for a ceremonial parade. People passing by must have thought I was trying to get an early discharge on mental health grounds. Another job was to go around all the paths in the barrack complex and pick up any rubbish that might be lying about. I had to deposit this stuff into sacks and present it to the guard commander, who then ceremoniously dumped the contents of the sacks into the dustbin adjacent to the guardroom.

After a two-day settling-in period, we were introduced to the drill square. Imagine the picture presented by thirty-six recruits attempting for the first time to march in unison. On the command 'Quick march!' some started off with both arms swinging together, others went off right foot first, some almost went

Part of the drill square today. The square has been landscaped and the barracks converted to private accommodation.

off both feet forward at the same time. It was as a shambles. Yet it only took a few parades under the lashing tongue of the drill sergeant to bring a semblance of order to the proceedings. In a few weeks we were marching at the regulation pace of 140 paces per minute and 160 per minute quick-time for ceremonial parades.

The reason we were not allowed out of the barracks during the first four weeks of training was to ensure that when we did eventually go into town, we would not let down the regiment. On my first outing, however, I certainly let myself down – both literally and metaphorically. I had formed a friendship with one particular chap and we decided to venture forth and take our first look at

The statue of King Alfred in Winchester High Street.

the ancient capital of Wessex. We stepped out smartly and headed towards the statue of King Alfred the Great. On the other side of the road, we spotted what we thought was an officer coming towards us, and as we had been instructed that at all times we must salute an officer, we prepared to put the order into practice. On the approach of the supposed officer, we smartly turned our heads to the left and with some vigour swung our right arm up in a salute. The force of energy that I put into this manoeuvre caused my feet to slip from under me and down I went, landing on my bottom with my hand still in the saluting position staring up at the good King Alfred. The supposed officer crossed the road, stood over me and said, 'There's no need to salute me, sonny. I'm the Regimental Sergeant Major. An officer wears a tie. I have my collar buttoned up.'

We found Winchester to be an interesting and beautiful city. It boasted an eleventh-century cathedral, a Norman castle, and a famous public school. It also housed the depot of the Royal Hampshire Regiment as well as the two regiments already mentioned. The local people were very pleasant and we spent many very happy hours during our nine months in Winchester.

Inside the rifle depot we had quite a lot to squeeze into a day. There was physical training (more about that later), drill parades twice a day, rifle shooting practice on the range every day, and also revolver and machine-gun practice. On alternate Saturday mornings we had a 5-mile route march; on

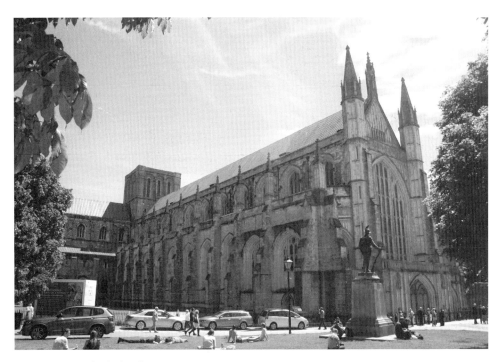

Winchester Cathedral today.

Statue of a rifleman outside Winchester Cathedral.

the other Saturday we had a 5-mile cross-country run. After three months, the route march was extended to 10 miles, and after six months we had to march 15 miles in full marching order. This consisted of a full backpack, side haversack, full water bottle, rifle and bayonet.

Some chaps with a natural flair for gymnastics enjoyed the training sessions but others like me dreaded the thought of the gymnasium. The army in those days seemed to attract the worst type of bully to the position of Physical Training Instructor. They would place drawing pins on the far end of the vaulting horse in order to encourage you to clear the end. Another favourite ploy was to make us climb ropes suspended from the ceiling, and if we failed to reach the top they would throw Swedish drill clubs up and hit us on the legs. As a consequence of this, we returned to terra firma a lot quicker than we went up. But I suppose all these things had the desired effect. It certainly smartened and toughened us up and at the conclusion of the nine months' training we felt a very professional outfit indeed.

By the end of 1932, I had obtained my Army Certificate of Education Third Class and Second Class. Second Class involved examinations in English, map reading, mathematics and 'army and empire'. A red-letter day for us was 5 January 1933 – the day of our passing-out parade before the Colonel-in-Chief

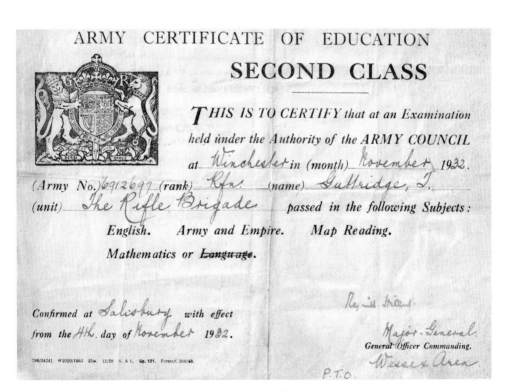

Tom passed his Army Certificate of Education Second Class in November 1932.

of the Regiment, the Duke of Connaught. For several days it was all go: plenty of spit and polish. On the morning of 5 January, we had four inspections prior to the actual parade. Section Leader, Platoon Commander, Company Commander, and finally the Commanding Officer of the Regiment all passed up and down the ranks searching for any flaws in the general turnout. Even the studs on our boots had to be burnished to a brilliant shine, and the back of the cap badge had to be as highly polished as the front.

The Duke arrived with a retinue of top brass – one brigadier, two aides-de-camp (ADCs), and a complement of colonels. After inspecting the ranks, the Duke took his place on the rostrum ready for the ceremonial part of the parade. For this occasion, we had accompanying us the full drum and bugle band of the 1st Battalion of the Rifle Brigade, from their barracks in Devonport. It was quite inspiring walking to such tunes as *Marching Through Georgia* and other well-known Sousa marches. We marched and counter-marched, finally finishing with the ceremonial march-past and double march-past. These latter two were performed at 140 and 160 paces per minute.

The day following the passing-out parade was spent on the rifle range. This was another important day for us, as it meant that we either qualified as marksmen with the rifle, revolver and machine gun, or we failed to reach the required standard. In the latter event, you would have to remain at Winchester until such time as you finally did qualify. The same standard also applied at the drill passing-out parade. If you failed to impress, it meant staying on at the depot for at least another three months. Not a happy thought. Only two chaps failed to make the grade, however, and a few days later we received instructions to join the First Battalion, stationed at the North Raglan Barracks, Devonport. First, however, we were granted seven days' leave and issued with two railway warrants, one from Winchester to Waterloo, the other from Waterloo to Plymouth. The seven days passed all too quickly, and on the seventh we all congregated at Waterloo station ready to board the Plymouth Express. The single fair from Waterloo to Plymouth in 1933 was £1. I remember it well because although I did not have to pay it on this first occasion, I did on many others.

The second chapter of my army life, the time at Devonport, was to be a fairly short one, but hectic and eventful nonetheless. The Raglan Barrack complex consisted of a very large drill square, some 300 yards in length and 100 yards wide. There were large blocks of buildings at each end of the square. These consisted of officers' quarters, troops' quarters, and administration offices with an exact duplication of the layout at the other end. The north end of this set-up was known as North Raglan Barracks and was occupied by the Rifle Brigade; the other end, South Raglan Barracks, was occupied by the First Battalion the South Wales Borderers (SWBs).

We did not experience the bustle and chaos that we were subjected to in our early days at Winchester. Now, there was a professional feel about our activities. Drill parades went with a swing; the heavy sound of marching boots and the harsh sounds of commands from the mouths of drill sergeants at both ends of the square were a regular feature from Monday to Friday. On Sundays we had a combined church parade with the SWBs. Both regiments would march through the town led by their respective bands – drum and bugle for the Rifle Brigade, drum and fife for the SWB. The citizens of Devonport lined the pavements to witness the march past.

A few weeks after our arrival we were initiated into the art of traffic duty. We spent several days acting as understudies to the civilian police, learning how to control the traffic in Union Street. The traffic in those days, of course, was nothing like as heavy as it is today. But it was interesting work and we enjoyed the day when our turn came around to assist the police.

Being close to Dartmoor, much of our time was taken up with army manoeuvres, and on some occasions we spent three or four nights on the moor under canvas. Dartmoor can be an eerie, haunting place at night, and night patrols or guard duty in the damp swirling mist of the moor, with the occasional cry of a wild animal, stood us in good stead for events that were to happen later on. Once, during a night patrol, we heard a siren sound across the moor. This was a warning to all that a prisoner had escaped from the forbidding Dartmoor Prison. Very few men made a successful break, the majority becoming trapped in the marshy bogs. On the occasion of the Dartmoor Mutiny – a prison riot in 1932 – our regiment had mounted guard outside the gates and perimeter walls.

In those days, between the two world wars, Great Britain had a sizeable navy, and Plymouth and Devonport, with their respective docks and port facilities, were bustling hives of activity. Three months after arriving at Devonport, I was posted to the signal platoon of HQ Company and was soon involved in the intricacies of Morse code, flag semaphore and heliograph lamp signalling. The Royal Navy signallers were experts in all types of signalling, and the two services had an arrangement whereby the army signallers joined the navy boys for tuition and polishing to a higher standard than you normally reached in the army. By the time I eventually left Devonport, I had the crossed flags of a fully qualified signaller on the left arm of my jacket, together with the crossed rifles surrounded by a laurel wreath denoting that I was a marksman with rifle and revolver.

We had plenty of time for sport and the battalion had a reasonably strong soccer team playing in the Plymouth and District League. Every other Saturday afternoon, however, we made our way to Home Park, the ground of Plymouth Argyle. At that time they were a Division One club. The regiment had one player, Vic Maudie, who went on to play for Plymouth Argyle and later for Charlton

Athletic. We still had our 15-mile route marches and cross-country runs to contend with on Saturday mornings, but being fit, they did not cause us any problems.

Towards the end of September 1933, the battalion received orders that on 1 November we were to embark on the troopship *Neuralia* for posting to St Andrew's Barracks, Malta. The next two months became a period of high excitement and feverish activity. Everyone was kitted out with subtropical uniform including lightweight khaki drill jackets, shorts, knee-length stockings and pith helmets. There was a period of leave beforehand but the time passed quickly and it was with mixed feelings that we said goodbye to our families and friends before making our way back to Devonport for a final flurry of activity prior to entraining for Southampton.

Tom in subtropical uniform.

CHAPTER 2

ISLAND INTERLUDE

At 7 a.m. on 31 October 1933, we left our barracks for the last time and headed for Plymouth station, led by the regimental band. The journey to Southampton took several hours, with a long break at Salisbury for a meal. We finally arrived at our destination at 5 p.m. and assembled on the dockside, below the already lowered walkways of the troopship *SS Neuralis*, a vessel of approximately 10,000 tons. Although it appeared to be a large ship when viewed from the dockside, once on board it turned out to be a very different proposition. There were already several other battalions of troops on board, some bound for Gibraltar, others on their way to India. By the time we were shown our quarters below deck and each issued with a hammock, there was little room to move.

This view of Valletta has changed little since this picture was taken in the 1930s.

The first day at sea was fairly uneventful, although it was depressing to see the coastline of the British Isles growing fainter and finally disappearing altogether. The sea was reasonably calm until we entered the mouth of the Bay of Biscay. This was to be our introduction to rock 'n' roll. The ship heaved violently from side to side and bucked and reared like a rocking horse. Hundreds of men could be seen leaning over the side being violently seasick and wishing they were dead. Fortunately this never happened to me – I remained completely unaffected throughout the entire voyage, possibly because I continually chewed dry biscuits. This was a tip I had been given by an old sailor.

Off the Portuguese coast we passed groups of fishing boats trawling for sardines and pilchards. The sea swell was so high that on several occasions these small boats entirely disappeared from our sight, lost in a vast trough of water, only to reappear high above us on the crest of a wave.

It took around two-and-a-half days to reach Gibraltar but our stay was a short one, as the only people authorised to disembark were the troops whose destination was The Rock. Then it was non-stop to Malta, another 1,000 miles and another two-and-a-half days' sailing. Around 900 men had left the ship at Gibraltar, so there was much more room for the rest of us and we were more able to relax and watch the schools of dolphins enjoying themselves in the blue waters of the Mediterranean Sea. The sea was as calm as a millpond and we quite enjoyed the contrast with the first two-and-a-half days. For several hours we hugged the North African coastline, passing such places as Algiers and Oran in Algeria and Bizerta in Tunisia.

Towards the evening of our fifth day at sea, we sighted a small group of islands. These turned out to be Malta, Gozo and Comino. Our voyage was nearly over and a new adventure lay before us. There was much hustle and bustle aboard as we prepared to disembark. Those left on board and bound for destinations further afield, such as Aden and India, were no doubt pleased to see the back of us, as it would mean more room for them on board.

My first view of Malta was the imposing Grand Harbour. This was almost completely filled with ships of the Royal Navy including several battleships with names like *Revenge, Repulse, Resolution* and *Renown*. Each was armed with 15-inch guns capable of hitting their target at a range of 20 miles. Accompanying these dreadnoughts were cruisers, destroyers, minesweepers and all the other auxiliary ships that go to make up a fleet. To the left as you entered the harbour were the ramparts and formidable fortifications guarding access. These defences were manned by lines of heavy artillery under the control of the Royal Malta Artillery.

The island of Malta covers an area of only 122 square miles – smaller even than the Isle of Wight (144 square miles). Despite its size, it was a very important and strategic naval base, situated around halfway along

Royal Navy ships at anchor.

St Andrew's Barracks, Malta, where Tom was based from 1933–38.

Inspection by General Sir David Campbell, St Andrew's Barracks, 1933.

the Mediterranean. Malta was annexed by Britain in 1814 and gained its independence in 1964. As a result it ceased to be a British naval base and all naval and military personnel left the island. At the time of my sojourn on the island, however, it was a hive of naval and military activity. The British army on the island at that time consisted of one battalion from each of two infantry regiments. The other one was the Cheshire Regiment. In addition the Royal Malta Artillery manned the Grand Harbour defences. This regiment was made up of British officers and Maltese other ranks. The Rifle Brigade was situated in St Andrew's Barracks, high on a hill overlooking Sliema Bay. The Cheshire Regiment was accommodated in St George's Barracks much lower down the hill, almost level with the bay itself.

The capital of Malta is Valletta, and for the services the street known as Strada Street was the main attraction. The name, I recall, meant 'Street of Steps'. The road and pavement were so narrow, only around 5 feet across, and they were made up of steps going steeply up for around 100 yards. The main feature of the street, though, was the continuous formation of nightclubs and bars down both sides. The hostesses in these establishments were girls from countries all over the world – Germany, Poland, Hungary, Egypt and Japan. Strangely enough, there were very few from the British Isles. Of an evening, 'the Street', as it was known, became a milling mass of service personnel, especially sailors.

Mosta Church, Malta, boasts the world's third largest unsupported dome. During the Second World War it was famously penetrated by a German bomb during a service but the device failed to explode.

The Roman Catholic Church had a very strong influence over the Maltese people and almost daily somewhere on the island there would be a colourful procession wending its way through the narrow streets. In whichever village the religious procession was taking place, work was abandoned for the day. The Maltese had more religious holidays than anywhere else in the world, more even than Spain.

Another notable sight on Malta in those days was the large herds of goats that wandered the streets, each goat with a bell attached to its neck. The goats were the island's equivalent of our United Dairies. We became accustomed to the tinkling sound of perhaps fifty jangling bells, all sending out their message at the same time. There were no cattle on the island and there was very little grass. Service personnel were forbidden to drink goat's milk as it could cause undulant fever, a bacterial disease whose symptoms include fevers, myalgia and back pain. The Maltese people were immune to undulant fever but for those not brought up on the local milk it could be fatal.

Service life on the island in those days before the Second World War can only be described as idyllic. There was plenty of time for swimming in the blue waters of the Med and pollution was unheard of at that time. There was cricket in the spring and football in the winter and polo for the officers. Of course, it was not all play – we had physical training every day and weapon

Tom (far left) enjoying Maltese beach life with some of his friends.

ARMY CERTIFICATE OF EDUCATION

FIRST CLASS

THIS IS TO CERTIFY that at an Examination held in March, 1937, at MALTA, *under the Authority of the ARMY COUNCIL,*

No. 6912697 Rifleman THOMAS REGINALD GUTTRIDGE, The Rifle Brigade,

passed in English, Mathematics, Geography and Map Reading.

To take effect from the 17th March, 1937.

_____ *General Staff.*

Major General, Director of Military Training.

(33547) W1. 20876 3300 9/36 Hw. G.620 J.3337

Tom passed his First Class Education Certificate in 1937.

training to follow. I also spent part of each day studying for my first-class Army Certificate of Education. This involved English, maths, geography and map-reading, and I passed all these subjects in 1937. We also had our usual quota of route marches and cross-country runs, so our days were fully occupied.

My favourite spot on the island was St Paul's Bay, so named because this was supposed to be the spot where St Paul came ashore when he visited the island. I would just sit on the rocks in the cool of the late afternoon, listening to the sound of the waves lapping my feet, sometimes reading a book, sometimes just letting my mind travel to imagine the day St Paul landed here. The bay itself must have changed very little since those early days of Christianity. The very place instilled in you an atmosphere of history and times past. It is hard to explain, but I always left St Paul's Bay with a feeling of well-being.

In the spring of 1934, we were invited to put our names forward for a chance to join the summer cruise with the First Battle Squadron of the Mediterranean Fleet. I had the good fortune to be selected and joined *HMS Revenge* on 10 October following her arrival in Malta after joint exercises with the Atlantic Fleet. There were twenty soldiers allotted to the *Revenge*, and a similar number

Catching up on the news from home with the *East London Advertiser*.

to *HMS Renown*, *HMS Resolution*, and the other destroyers and auxiliary ships that made up the full complement for the cruise. Leaving the Grand Harbour, we headed east towards the Adriatic. Our first port of call was the Greek island town of Argostoli.

During the voyage we were given conducted tours of the working parts of the ship and were even allowed to stand in the 15-inch gun turrets while the guns were being fired in practice. This was an impressive experience. The shells, each weighing a ton, arrived in the turret from the bowels of the ship by means of hydraulic lifts. When loaded and fired, the recoil of the gun was 1 yard. Onlookers were protected by a brass rail situated 2 yards back from the gun barrel. The accurate range of these guns was between 20 and 25 miles.

While anchored off Argostoli, we were given the chance to try our hand at rowing in the ship's whaleboat. This had a rowing crew of eight and its main task was to ferry men from the ship to the landing stage at any port of call. The boat itself was rather large and cumbersome, and besides the crew it had to accommodate twenty passengers. Not being used to rowing, we found the going very hard and tiring. We enjoyed two days on this island and then headed for the beautiful island of Corfu. In those days these islands were unspoilt by tourists and the trappings of modern commercialism.

Corfu was a fabulous place as also were our next two ports of call, Kotor and Split. Those towns are respectively in Montenegro and Croatia today but

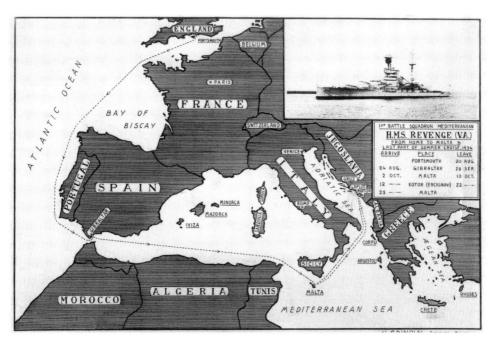

The route taken by HMS *Revenge* during her summer cruise in 1934. Tom joined the ship at Malta in October.

in 1934 we were in Yugoslavian waters. While anchored off the harbour of Split, news came through of the assassination of the King of Yugoslavia, King Alexander. He had been gunned down while on a diplomatic visit to France and his body was returned to his homeland on board a Yugoslav cruiser. The British First Battle Squadron formed a double line and the cruiser carrying the King's body passed through the middle. The crews of the British ships lined the decks in full parade dress and as the cruiser passed, each ship fired a salute from a 4-inch gun.

After Split, we visited Gruz and the old medieval city of Dubrovnik (now in Croatia). This beautiful old walled city was said to rival Venice in the sixteenth century. Its foremost attraction is the marvellous seventeenth-century cathedral, built after its medieval predecessor was destroyed in an earthquake in 1667. Even in 1934, Dubrovnik was popular with tourists and a favourite meeting place of the Prince of Wales (later King Edward VIII) and his future wife, Mrs Wallis Simpson.

I'm ashamed to say that during one evening trip into Dubrovnik I blotted my copybook. A party of us – soldiers and Royal Marines – went ashore to partake of a little light refreshment. Some of us had a few too many and, not being completely in control of our senses, we boarded the whaleboat attached to *HMS Resolution* instead of the one for the *Revenge*. We had to sleep on

A fly-past, probably in 1930s Malta.

deck for the remainder of the night, and next morning we were hauled up before the captain and given a right rocket. We were also informed that the *Revenge* had already left Dubrovnik and was heading back towards Malta. We arrived back at our base in late November and, as expected, were not too popular. Our Commanding Officer had plenty to say about letting down the name of the regiment. No further action was taken, however.

We settled back into the normal routine of drill, weapon training and route marches. In 1936, however, world events brought a sudden change to our ordered way of life. Benito Mussolini, the Italian dictator, had declared war against Abyssinia in the latter half of 1935, and the following year he overcame the resistance of the Abyssinians, whose country was occupied by Italian troops. The Emperor of Abyssinia (now Ethiopia) was Haile Selassie, and just before his country was occupied, he fled into exile in England. On his way he stopped off in Malta and I had the privilege of being a member of the guard of honour detailed to receive him when he stepped ashore from the British cruiser taking him to England.

During the Abyssinian War, Mussolini threatened on several occasions to invade Malta. Relations between the United Kingdom and Italy were at their lowest ebb due to our support for the Emperor, and life on the island became quite hectic. We were ordered to seal off all possible landing sites for an invasion force with barbed-wire entanglements and pillbox gun emplacements situated in the most strategic positions to deter an enemy. However, after the final collapse of the Ethiopian forces, life returned to normal.

The year 1936 had more history in the making, however. One thousand miles west of Malta, the Spaniards were becoming involved in their civil war. General Francisco Franco had risen to power before the war and led the fascist revolt with German and Italian support, becoming head of the insurgent government. At this time I had another opportunity to go to sea with the Royal Navy. I was detailed to join *HMS Grenville* for a three-week cruise and combined operations with the Atlantic Fleet. This ship was named after the sixteenth-century seaman Sir Richard Grenville, who was responsible for carrying the first colonists to Virginia. The *Grenville* was a destroyer flotilla leader, much smaller than *HMS Revenge*, as a result of which I did not ride the waves so well. I also found conditions on board rather cramped and restricted.

I was now a member of the Signal Platoon of Headquarters Company and the primary reason for my being on this cruise was to brush up on all types of signalling – semaphore, Morse code and heliograph (lamp signalling). Our first destination was Gibraltar, where we were to rendezvous with vessels of the Home Fleet before taking part in Atlantic Ocean manoeuvres.

Whilst in Gibraltar Harbour we were close to the fringes of the war in Spain. We heard occasional gunfire and witnessed aerial activity overhead. At one stage it was thought by the powers that be that we were being threatened. The presence of Spanish aircraft overhead prompted orders to 'adopt battle

HMS *Greyhound* in the Mediterranean in 1934.

Military parades in 1930s Malta.

stations'. This meant being put into a state of readiness and being battened down in case retaliatory action was deemed necessary.

It was only a precaution, and conditions soon returned to normal. We did see a large number of refugees crossing from Spain into Gibraltar. We eventually left the harbour and headed out into the Atlantic. Again I found myself in the thick of some really awful weather in the Bay of Biscay. Huge waves leapt high over the bows of the destroyer and over half the ship's company were seasick. Again I escaped this torment. I enjoyed life at sea and often wished that I had joined the Royal Navy instead of the army. The fleet manoeuvres in the Atlantic took us to within 25 miles of the English coast: so near and yet so far after being overseas for two years! There was too much action and activity, however, to find time for homesickness.

Being once again back on Malta after three weeks at sea seemed at first to be rather dull, but with plenty to do, life soon settled back into the old routine. At around this time we had a surfeit of first-class sporting personalities visiting the island. The then famous Hungarian soccer team Ferencvaros were touring the Mediterranean, playing matches in Malta, Italy and Greece. The best team in Malta was Sliema Wanderers, a squad of mixed nationalities. The team included four players from the English or Scottish leagues, two from France, one from Italy, while the remainder were young Maltese players. They were no match for the Hungarians, who ran out winners by 13 goals to 1. The Sliema goalkeeper was Jock McTaggart, who in his younger days had played for Hibernian in the Scottish First Division. He was heard to remark after the match that it had been a back-breaking experience, and one he did not wish to repeat. I remember that the Hungarian centre forward scored seven goals. His name was Dr Sarosi and he was an international.

Another sportsman to visit the island at around this time was Joe Davis, the world-famous billiards champion. He was touring the world to play in exhibition matches. Billiards in those days was far more popular than snooker.

When I joined the army I had signed on for a period of seven years with the Colours and five years on the Reserve. In March 1939, my seven years were almost at an end. I was detailed to return home on board the *SS California* as an ordinary second-class passenger, along with a detachment of other chaps also due for discharge. The voyage home was a holiday in itself. We had little to do but sun ourselves. We had two-berth cabins and dined in the main restaurant along with the other passengers. We had an arrangement with the catering staff that we could have extras if we so wished. Needless to say, we so wished.

The ship's destination in the United Kingdom was the port of Glasgow, and this was another new experience for me, sailing up the Irish Sea and up the River Clyde to Scotland's biggest port. We passed all the large shipbuilding yards, such as John Brown's, where the large ocean-going liners were built, and finally came

A rowing crew in Malta Harbour.

into the docks ahead of disembarkation. The ship's passenger list was made up of ordinary civilians, business people and service personnel and their families, returning from such outposts of empire as India, Singapore and the Middle East.

We lined up to leave the ship, our baggage of kitbag and other equipment having already been put ashore to await our collection. Our turn came eventually to walk down the gangway and place our feet on to British soil for the first time in five years. I was around three-quarters of the way down the gangway when a photographer suddenly thrust a woman carrying a baby in my direction so it appeared that we were together. He then asked me to hold the baby for 'just a minute' and snapped the camera. Later that day the picture appeared in the *Glasgow Evening News* under the headline 'Married families arrive from India'. I never did learn where the lady's husband was but I doubt that he would have been too happy to see the photograph.

After a brief 'cheerio' to several shipboard acquaintances, our small detachment boarded an army lorry and was taken to Maryhill Barracks for a meal and a bed for the night. In 1939 this part of Glasgow was one of the poorer areas of the city. On the journey from the docks we saw many signs of squalor – tall tenement buildings housing many poor families, children roaming the streets barefoot, roads unswept, and filth in all the gutters. There seemed to be a general air of gloom.

Our stay in Glasgow was brief and the next day we entrained for our final destination, Tidworth in Hampshire. As I was due for discharge and transfer to the Reserve, I did not anticipate being too long at Tidworth, and so it turned out. Within a few days the paperwork was completed and I returned to civilian life, although technically I had another six weeks as a soldier while I took the six weeks' leave owed to me. My stay in 'civvy street', however, was to be all too short-lived.

FIRST   BATTALION

THE RIFLE BRIGADE
(PRINCE CONSORT'S OWN)

PRESENTED TO

No. *6912697* Rank *Rifleman*

Name *T. R. Cultridge*

On his leaving the Battalion

C. Hoskyns

Lt.-Colonel
Commanding 1st Bn. The Rifle Brigade

The certificate presented to Tom when he left the Rifle Brigade for the first time in 1939.

CHAPTER 3

WAR CLOUDS

It was the summer of 1939 and war clouds were gathering. My leave had officially ended in May but in July I received my call-up papers and a railway warrant for a one-way journey. As a soldier on the Reserve, I was ordered to report back to Tidworth within six days. In the meantime I also received a letter from my friend Jack Mallon, an Irishman from Belfast. Jack and I had been mates since our early Malta days and had resolved to keep in touch following our discharge. I knew Jack was working as a labourer on the Southern Railway in Hampshire but his latest letter told me that he too had been ordered to report to Tidworth. We were looking forward to meeting up again but when I reported for duty, there was no sign of Jack. I then received news via the Orderly Room that he had been killed saving a fellow railway worker's life. They were working on the Waterloo–Plymouth line at Fleet when an express train caught them unawares. Jack managed to push his colleague clear of the train but had no time to save himself. He had died a hero but the news upset me for some time.

Following my arrival at Tidworth I was appointed Orderly Room Corporal, a role that placed me at the very hub of the regiment. Despite Prime Minister Neville Chamberlain's declarations about 'Peace in our time', it was evident from information coming through that war was not far away. It became all but inevitable on 1 September when Germany invaded Poland. As the UK had a treaty with Poland, we were left with no alternative but to declare war. At 11 a.m. two days later, I and other members of the administration team gathered around our Listen radio in the orderly room to hear the historic announcement that 'Britain is at war with Germany'. I can still recall the air of suppressed excitement when the full portent of the news was realised by those present.

For the next two weeks Tidworth became a hive of activity as the regiment was placed on a war footing. The Rifle Brigade and our sister regiment, the Kings Royal Rifle Corps, together with a territorial regiment, the Queen Victoria Rifles, were formed into a composite unit and became the support group of the First Armoured Division. We then, for the next two weeks, embarked on a period of intense infantry training and manoeuvres on Salisbury Plain.

The first wartime intake of recruits at Winchester Barracks in September 1939. (Photo: Hampshire Record Office: The Royal Green Jackets Archive: 170A12W/D/2208/24)

After this we received orders to proceed to Blandford Forum in Dorset. This was my introduction to a rural county that was to become my home in later years. The inhabitants greeted us with great friendliness. The KRRC were billeted in Sturminster Newton and the QV Rifles in the village of Milton Abbas.

Our short stay in Blandford was mainly spent in bringing all our equipment and vehicles up to scratch after the exercises on Salisbury Plain. After only three weeks there, our commanding officer received 'sealed orders' to entrain the regiment on a special train at Blandford station. Three days after receiving our orders to move, the regiment formed up in the station approach and at 7 p.m. we set off for destination unknown. We travelled for mile after mile through hours of darkness, not knowing where we were heading or even in which direction. After some twelve hours in daylight, we arrived at our first destination – Stranraer, a west coast port in Scotland. It was fairly obvious that we were heading for Northern Ireland. Our commanding officer had by now opened his sealed orders and confirmed to us that our destination was Banbridge in County Down.

We made the short sea crossing to Larne in around one hour and proceeded by road to Banbridge. All our equipment and vehicles had followed us in a goods train and we were reunited with them at Larne. Our destination was supposed to be a closely guarded secret but on our arrival at Stranraer we were told that William Joyce, aka Lord Haw Haw, the voice of German propaganda, had announced details of our journey in his morning radio tirade that day. As we had left Blandford under sealed orders with even the CO not knowing our

Blandford in the 1940s. (Photo: Barry Cuff Collection)

Blandford railway station. (Photo: Barry Cuff Collection)

destination, the leak must have originated in the War Office in Whitehall. It is hard to reach any other conclusion.

Banbridge was a small, pleasant market town situated on the banks of the River Bann, between the two much larger towns of Portadown and Downpatrick. It nestles in a valley within sight of the Mountains of Mourne. It was a delightful place and the locals made us very welcome, and often invited us into their houses for a glass of real Irish Guinness and a slice of soda bread. Some of us went by train to Belfast in the evenings and during one of these excursions we met up with nurses from the Royal Victoria Hospital.

Our stay was far too short for any serious friendships to develop. The IRA were active at that time, although not on the scale that we were to see in later decades. The Royal Ulster Constabulary kept things under control. We had to be constantly on guard, though, and for a football match against Glentoran we had two machine guns strategically placed at the ground. This area was known as a hotbed of IRA activity.

Most of our two-month stay in the province was taken up with small arms training at Ballykinler Firing Ranges near Newry. It was here that a few of us did a rather foolish thing that could later have landed us in serious trouble. We had been practising firing with our gas masks on but they kept misting up, giving us a very poor view of the target. Someone had the bright idea of removing the eyeglasses from the gas masks. It certainly improved our vision but unfortunately we forgot to replace them afterwards; and even had we done so, they would no longer have been well enough sealed to protect us.

At the end of two months we were again on the move, this time in reverse order – Banbridge to Larne, ferry to Stranraer, then train back to Dorset. This time we were billeted in two villages around 2 and 3 miles outside Blandford, namely, Charlton Marshall and Spetisbury. My sleeping quarters were in the Old Rectory opposite Charlton Marshall church. Our hostess was a Mrs Phillips, widow of a former rector of the parish. The house was detached with an extensive garden containing a tennis court. The girls from Blandford Telephone Exchange played on this court regularly and it was not long before we started making friends and spending many happy evenings in their company.[1] One young lady immediately caught my eye and, although the

---

1 With help from Charlton Marshall village historian Mark Churchill, the house where Tom was billeted has been identified as Charlton Cottage, which is indeed almost opposite the church. Mark says it never was an 'Old Rectory' in the full sense but was the home of the Revd Frank Benet Phillips and his wife in the 1920s and 1930s and that Mr Phillips acted as Curate of the parish for a while. He had presumably died by 1940. The tennis court has been lawned but its borders can still be made out and the present owner, Robert Harman, says the original hardcore survives beneath the grass.

Charlton Marshall parish church.

attraction did not at first appear to be mutual, she did consent to my walking
her home to Blandford. It was not long before we were seeing each other on
a regular basis. Connie Ridout, the young lady in question, eventually became
my wife. This was several years later, however. Much else was to unfold before
that became possible.

   After six or seven weeks in the Blandford area, as the 'phoney war' ended
and Hitler's forces advanced into the Low Countries, we were again on the
move. This was early April 1940, and our orders from the War Office were
to proceed to East Anglia and set up defences in order to repel an invasion.
I was on a few days' leave and visiting my family in Dulwich, London, when
a telegram arrived ordering me back to Charlton Marshall 'at the double'. On
my return, I was surprised to find that the battalion had already left for the first
rendezvous at Bury St Edmunds in Suffolk. Together with other late arrivals,
I boarded a 3-ton army lorry, kindly left for us by the transport section, and
off we went in an attempt to catch up with the main body of the regiment. We
left in such a hurry that we had no time to say goodbye to our girlfriends or the
villagers. The girls, being telephone operators, knew that we had gone, but not

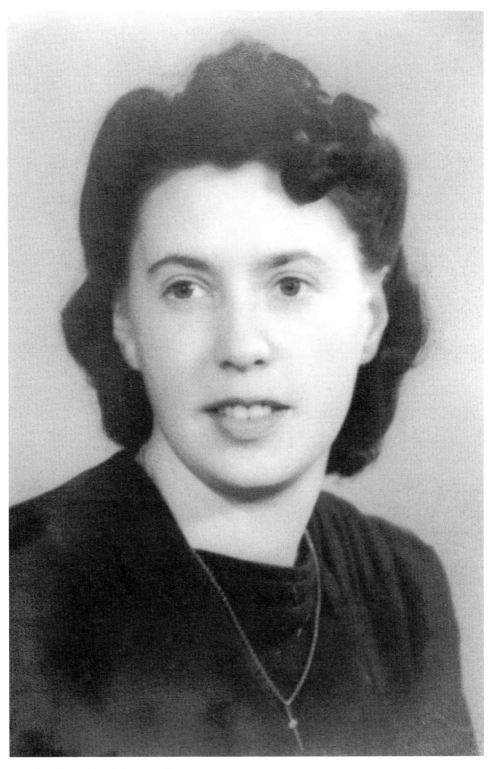

Connie Ridout, Tom's future wife.

the destination. As events turned out, it would be some years before we were able to communicate with one another again.

We caught up with our comrades at Bury St Edmunds some twenty-four hours later. No sooner had we arrived, however, than the CO received fresh orders and we found ourselves on the road again, this time heading for Stowmarket, also in Suffolk. There seemed to be no rhyme nor reason for these moves but ours was not to reason why. It looked as if the suddenness of the German advance into Holland and Belgium had caught the powers that be on one leg and they appeared to be at sixes and sevens.

We stayed at Stowmarket for the best part of a week and our official mission was to repel invaders, who were expected to arrive on parachutes. They did not materialise, however, and life was generally peaceful and ordinary. It was hard to realise that there was a war on, but this was soon to change and the next ten days proved to be a turning point in my life.

During the second week of May 1940, we received orders to leave Stowmarket and proceed 'with all despatch' to Southampton, and there to rendezvous with the remainder of the First Armoured Division Support Group, namely, the King's Royal Rifle Corps and the motorcycle battalion Territorial Unit, the Queen Victoria Rifles. It took us two full days and one night to reach

Charlton Cottage, where Tom was billeted in 1940.

Southampton. Our route took us through Ipswich, Colchester, Chelmsford, Leyton, and into London, then through Guildford and Winchester.

Southampton was a veritable hive of industry with troops and vehicles everywhere. Apparently the object of the exercise was for the First Armoured Division Support Group to embark at Southampton and disembark at Boulogne to give support to the Welsh Guards, who were already in action in that vicinity. However, events moved too quickly for these orders to be carried out. Boulogne was on the point of collapse. All our units were aboard ship when once again our orders were changed. We were now instructed to head for Dover and await further orders. It was 6 a.m. on 20 May when the convoy reached Dover. The KRRC and the QVRs embarked on the SS *Royal Daffodil* and the Rifle Brigade on *SS Archangel*. There was a lot of confusion when the arms and equipment of all three regiments was loaded on to a third ship, the SS *City of Canterbury*.

CHAPTER 4

INTO BATTLE

Our orders were to sail to Calais, engage the enemy and delay their advance towards Dunkirk as long as possible. We had barely reached mid-Channel when we came under attack for the first time. A German Heinkel bomber approached and dropped two bombs close to our ship before the anti-aircraft guns on the single escorting destroyer opened up and scared the intruder away. As we neared the French coast, we could already hear the sound of gunfire, which seemed to be coming from the shoreline between Calais and Boulogne. Shortly before we entered Calais harbour, our escorting destroyer dropped several depth charges after picking up the sound of an enemy submarine.

The Rifle Brigade went ashore at 2 p.m. on 20 May. Broken glass from the shattered windows of the railway station and other buildings in the vicinity of the docks littered the ground. There were piles of abandoned French army kit

One of eleven Calais photos in Tom's album, taken by a German soldier following the town's collapse.

lying about and bomb craters and debris were everywhere. The Rifle Brigade took up positions on the ridge of sandhills between the north side of the Bassin des Chasses and the seashore. There was no sign yet of the ship carrying our transport and ammunition. We had some small arms, such as rifles, bren guns and hand grenades, but no transport or heavy mortars.

We had hardly had time to settle down and get our bearings when the German shells began tearing into the harbour and railway marshalling yards. We watched as the shells fell on the far side of the harbour. The German artillery had got the range of the Gare Maritime. On the quay swarms of hysterical French people were crying in terror, 'Les Allemands, Les Allemands'. There was nothing much we could do until the vehicles and weapons arrived, so those who were not on duty just lay behind the sand dunes talking, smoking and brewing up tea. Someone said it was like Hyde Park on a bank holiday.

The two ships carrying the arms and equipment, SS *City of Canterbury* and SS *Kohistan*, arrived at 4 p.m. at low tide but there were no tugs available to tow them into port, so it was another two hours before they were finally able to dock and start unloading. At 5 p.m. Brigadier Nicholson, the officer commanding the Calais fighting force, issued his orders to the officers of all the regiments under his control. As the transport had not as yet been unloaded, the officers had to reach their respective units on foot. No one seemed to know exactly what was happening. Orders were being issued and then immediately countermanded. A rumour spread that there was to be a complete evacuation

An explosion tears through Calais.

of all personnel from Calais within the next twenty-four hours. Then it was announced that only the large number of wounded being brought into Calais by train would be embarked upon the *City of Canterbury* and the *Royal Daffodil*. In addition all non-fighting men were released from duty and ordered to embark on SS *Kohistan*. This ship was carrying most of the Rifle Brigade vehicles and ammunition, and in the general confusion, it sailed with the other two ships before being fully unloaded. This left the Rifle Brigade with very little ammunition. No one seemed particularly worried, however, as it was still believed that a full evacuation would take place.

We now know that the War Office wavered for some time about evacuating Calais, but by 23 May it had been decided that both Calais and Dunkirk must be held for as long as possible in order to evacuate the British Expeditionary Force (BEF) from Dunkirk. It was essential to get as many BEF troops out of Dunkirk as possible in order that we would have the nucleus of an army to build on and continue the fight. Had the BEF been wiped out in northern France, it is hard to see how Britain could have continued to stand up against Hitler.

Two Royal Navy ships, HMS *Gulzar* and HMS *Wessex*, were standing by a few miles offshore. At 9.33 a.m. on 24 May Brigadier Nicholson received a message from the Navy that only non-essential personnel would be evacuated. There would be no general evacuation and Calais was to be held for as long as possible at all costs. But the situation was changing hour by hour; orders and decisions were being made, then cancelled or reversed.

On that same morning, the Tenth Panzer Division of the German army commenced their attack on Calais. There had been skirmishes in and around

A column of wrecked vehicles at Calais.

The wreckage of a ship off the beach at Calais.

The remains of an artillery weapon.

the town for two or three days but this was to be their main assault. The KRRC C Company was surrounded and sustained heavy casualties. The Rifle Brigade were kept more or less pinned down all day by German snipers and long-range mortars. The trouble was that we had no long-range mortars with which to reply. We were also subjected to heavy bombardment by shells, mortars and dive-bombers, and casualties were heavy.

At 11.20 p.m. on 24 May, Brigadier Nicholson received a less-than-inspiring message from the Minister of War to the effect that Calais was to be held to the last man. 'This in accordance with regimental tradition – and the eyes of the Empire will be on you,' he was told. This message was underlined the following evening by another from Winston Churchill, who had become Prime Minister just two weeks earlier. At 9 p.m. on 25 May he told Brigadier Nicholson, 'Every hour you continue to exist is of the greatest help to BEF. The Government has therefore decided that you must continue to fight. Have greatest possible admiration for your splendid stand.' The two destroyers standing off Calais all day were withdrawn and returned to Dover, taking some of the early casualties with them. After midnight another destroyer entered the harbour with Vice-Admiral Sir James Somerville, whose mission was to discuss the defence of Calais with Brigadier Nicholson.

Damage as far as the eye can see.

The Rifle Brigade continued to hold the dock area, shoreline and sand dunes, while the KRRC were inland from the town. With our backs to the sea, the white cliffs of Dover within view and Panzer Divisions on three sides, it was probably inevitable that we still expected to be evacuated. This proved to be wishful thinking. The total garrison amounted to around 3,000 troops, mostly British and French but also some Belgians. The KRRC bore the brunt of the early action and took heavy casualties.

There was little sleep for anyone on the night of 25 May due to a continuous bombardment of mortars from the German lines. At 11.30 p.m. Brigadier Nicholson received a message from the War Office that the British 48th Division was on its way to relieve the small Calais garrison. This information turned out to be very misleading and disappointing to all in the hard-pressed garrison. When the message was sent, the 48th Division was pinned down by several Panzer battalions from two divisions on the other side of the Aa Canal. It wasn't very tactful to tell the commander of a beleaguered force that he was to hold to the death a town that was of no further importance to the BEF.

Despite the loss of more than half our transport and ammunition, the Rifle Brigade remained calm. There was an atmosphere of great tension – a

Shipping damage.

feeling of 'calm before the storm'. My small contribution to the war effort saw me initially with Battalion HQ situated on the northern rampart, near the Bastion 2 and immediately opposite Calais's Cellulose factory. The other companies of the Rifle Brigade were deployed in the following positions: HQ Company, less the Commanding Officer's staff, were dug in at Bastion 1 under the command of Major Coghill; this position was at the entrance to the tunnel under the fortress. A Company were holding a line from Bastion 4 to Bastion 2. C Company, under the command of Major Knollys, were situated at the blockhouse at the far eastern end of the Bassin des Chasses de l'Est. B Company under Major Hamilton-Russell were opposite battalion HQ but on the far side of the Cellulose factory. I Company, under Major Brush, held a line along the Canal de Calais. The whole of the Rifle Brigade was thus situated on the eastern side of Calais, while the King's Royal Rifle Corps were to the west of the town. The Queen Victoria Rifles were defending the area known as Calais St Pierre.

Early on the night of 25 May, we were dug in on the second sand ridge inland from the sea and facing the advancing Germans. It was beginning to get dark when we heard the sound of a lone aircraft approaching from the sea. It was a German Heinkel bomber. As it approached us, it let loose two large bombs. One landed on an open area of scrub and exploded harmlessly, causing quite a

Aerial view of maritime wreckage.

large crater. The other landed no more than 20 yards from our position but did not explode, instead sticking firmly in the sand. My immediate thought was that it was definitely not my turn yet!

After another long day, it was hard to resist the call of sleep, and I do remember dozing off, only to be rudely awakened by the sound of six Stukas, peeling off, diving and dropping bombs into the first sand ridge in from the sea. The noise of the explosions was terrific. We expected them to wheel round and bomb our sand ridge but instead they carried straight on and this was the last we saw of them. Another lucky escape!

The heat and noise were constant and by the morning of 26 May lack of sleep had dulled the senses to everything except holding our positions and stopping the enemy advance. The struggle raged at the canal front and in the harbour approaches. Twice during the early morning planes flew over dropping leaflets inviting us to surrender, but both times Brigadier Nicholson refused. At around 12 noon shells began falling in the vicinity of Rifle Brigade HQ. One shell found its mark and Lieutenant Colonel Hoskyns, our CO, was seriously wounded and later died.

After this episode, the HQ never really functioned again and HQ personnel, including myself, were deployed to other companies in order to reinforce their numbers. I joined a detachment of I Company under the command of Major P. Brush. I Company had started with 150 men but the number had now been reduced to one officer and seventy men. The officer, Major Brush, was an indomitable character, who had already been wounded twice – in the throat and in the neck – but refused to give in and was a shining example to his men. We had taken up a position in the marshalling yards of the railway and were endeavouring to shoot down two German snipers who were firing from a crane some distance away. I had been in this position for some time when Major Brush ordered Sergeant Phillips and me to take up a position opposite the Cellulose factory in order to try and silence a sniper who was shooting from the top floor. Only a few minutes after I left my original position, the unfortunate chap who had taken my place in the railway yard had his head blown clean off by a mortar bomb. Men kept turning the head over to try and see who it was. I, Sergeant Phillips and two other men used up what ammunition we had left and finally silenced the sniper. Whether he was killed, wounded, or discreetly withdrew, we never found out.

By this time everyone knew that the defence of Calais had entered its final day. By midday most of the town and outer suburbs had fallen. More or less the only ground still being held by the British and a handful of French was the dock area and shoreline, which we were still defending from the sand dunes. The aerial bombing had ceased but the shelling resumed, and this was followed by the advance of tanks and infantry. The advancing German

German troops check out the remains of a ship.

infantry appeared from the direction of the town centre and moved towards us without much thought of taking cover. Those of us who had some ammunition left were able to pick them off at will. But their superiority in numbers finally overwhelmed us. There was a minute or two of hand-to-hand fighting and I received a bayonet wound in my left arm, at the back of the elbow. It could have been worse, though. The only 'weapon' I had left was a tin of bully-beef and I instinctively threw this at the advancing German soldier, causing him to misdirect his aim. Yet another escape.

The fighting was finally over by 6 p.m. on 26 May. We were completely encircled by tanks and infantry, rounded up and made to assemble in the dock area. The officer commanding the three German divisions attacking the French coast was General Guderian, but the commander of the tank division that captured Calais itself was Erwin Rommel, then merely the German equivalent in the rank of a brigadier.

At around this time Royal Navy ships began shelling the advancing German supply columns. We could hear the shells whistling over our heads, and couldn't help thinking what a great pity it was that the Navy had left it so late to engage the enemy. Still, that was in keeping with the whole operation.

German soldiers stride towards Calais's ruined dockside.

Surveying the damage at Calais on 27 May 1940.

The Germans had advanced so quickly through the Low Countries and France that the powers that be had no answer to it. Orders had been issued and then countermanded, and so it went on. It was left to the officers and men under their command to do their best, which they did. Little did we realise, however, that 26 May 1940 was to be the first day of five years in captivity.

Although in a way we were sacrificial, we had achieved our objective by delaying the German advance sufficiently to allow the evacuation of 338,000 men from the beaches of Dunkirk. Winston Churchill himself later summed up our contribution when he wrote, 'A great effort which I hope we shall never forget. It would not have been possible to have used Dunkirk as a point from which to evacuate the BEF and the First French Army without this stand. The most famous regiments in the British Army, they fought it out to the end. When I sent them into Calais I was sure they would do their duty, and they did. A fitting finish to their history. Requiescant. The historic name of Calais should be written once more on British hearts.'

CHAPTER 5

DESTINATION UNKNOWN

It was around 7 p.m. on 26 May when a long column of tired, scruffy, disheartened, and hungry soldiers began the long march away from the French coast. At the time, it seemed to me like a dream, as though it was happening to someone else. We were all so tired that we could not really take in the situation at all. After around two hours of marching, we were herded into a large church and allowed to sleep in the pews or on the floor. Everyone was too exhausted to worry too much about anything, and it was not until the next morning that the enormity of the events hit us.

PoWs are rounded up.

At 7 a.m. next morning, 27 May, we were once again on the march. Breakfast was a non-event. To be fair to the Germans, the organising of food for approximately 1,700 PoWs at such short notice was something they could hardly be blamed for. Some of us had oddments of food, such as biscuits or chocolate, and this was shared around where possible.

Our route inland from the coast was not as the crow flies. Due to German troop movements towards the coast and hundreds of French refugees, we were taken on a circuitous route from one town to the next, travelling around 25 miles a day. We had our first issue of food at noon on 27 May. This consisted of a third of a loaf of dark brown rye bread and a mug of water each.

On the afternoon of day two I had a stroke of luck. During a rest period a few of us were lounging on the grass at the roadside when we heard an altercation going on between two French soldiers. Voices were raised and eventually they came to blows. The argument seemed to be about a suitcase that was lying open on the ground. The contents appeared to be food. Another chap and I thought it was time to intervene in the dispute so, whilst the two Froggies were at each other's throats, we picked up the case and discreetly moved further up the column. Our luck was definitely in, as the case contained a quantity of chocolate, biscuits, French cigarettes, and a box of matches. We transferred the contents of the suitcase into our haversacks and threw the suitcase over a hedge.

We passed through many villages but, as I recall, the main towns on our route were Lille, Arras, Cambrai, and Valenciennes in France and Mons in Belgium. Some of us had been discussing the possibility of making a break for it and between Lille and Arras four of us managed to slip the column. We dodged down a farm track and into a small copse, which hid us from the road. Emerging at the far end of the wood, we found ourselves in front of a large farmhouse, which had been abandoned by the farmer and his family after being hit by shellfire. Most of the windows were shattered and there was a great shell-hole through the kitchen wall. We had a good look around the house but the only food we could find was several packets of macaroni sticks. The water had been cut off so we did not see much point in staying for any length of time. We spent one night there and moved on the next morning. By the late afternoon we were in another wood and lit a fire in order to try and bake the macaroni. Unfortunately, the smoke from the fire was spotted by a German patrol. Two of them came to investigate. We were taken by truck to rejoin the column, but at least we had saved ourselves 10 miles of marching.

It was 18 June when we reached Valenciennes. Some days we had marched 25 miles; on other days we had rested in the fields. I well remember one night when we were in a field. It had been raining all day and it was still tipping

French prisoners stream through France in June 1940.

down when darkness fell. The ground was too wet to lie down so we had to stand up all night. The night seemed endless and all we could do was wonder when it all was going to end and how. It was a relief when dawn came, the rain ceased and the sun came out to dry our battledress, which by this time was in a sorry state. The food situation had improved after the first week of the march and every third day we had an issue of thin lentil soup and a slice of brown bread. This was accompanied by a mug of mint tea. Some of us still had our razors and we found the mint tea useful for shaving. This was a practice that we were to adopt throughout our captivity. Mint tea was vile to drink but it had its uses, as hot water was non-existent.

I must mention another stroke of luck that fell my way. I had been suffering with severe toothache for several days, and on asking an English-speaking guard about the problem, he said he would find out from an officer what, if anything, could be done about it. He was true to his word, and later informed me that on our arrival at Mons, I would be taken under escort to a dentist. As it turned out, the dentist's wife was English and came from Birmingham. She was also the receptionist, so was the first person I came into contact with in the waiting room. The dentist duly removed my aching tooth and on my return to the waiting room his wife was waiting with a parcel of Belgian chocolate and French cigarettes. There was a similar parcel for the guard by way of a sweetener.

At Mons it was my turn to queue for the ration of soup and bread. A number of us took turns to stand in queues, as you had to get into line at least an hour before the issue. When the food was about to be dished out, the others would join the waiting line, but on this day the guards suddenly divided the column into two. Being in the first half waiting for the issue of food, I was split up from the rest of my party and we were marched away. Not only did we get no lunch but I never met up with any of my mates again until the end of the war.

By now the column of prisoners numbered several thousand, made up of various nationalities – British, French, Dutch, Belgian, and a small number of Norwegians. The original column had been roughly split in half, no account being taken of who was with whom. I and many others had been separated from our friends and we had to strike up new friendships. Being with a new group and not knowing any of them was quite a traumatic experience. I got into conversation with a chap much older than me. He was fifty-five and a cook in a Territorial regiment. He had been a PoW in Germany from 1917–18 during the First World War. By a remarkable coincidence, he was to end up in the very same camp that had housed him the first time around.

Our new column headed for Liege. The journey seemed to go on forever – 'just another 3 kilometres,' according to the German guards. At the end of those 3 kilometres, it would be the same story again. The roads were long and straight and lined with poplar trees. After Liege, we found ourselves at Maastricht on the Dutch side of the Netherlands' border with Germany. My vivid memory of this town was not as the location of Prime Minister John Major's famous treaty with the European Community but of the generosity of its citizens. All along the High Street on both sides of the road heading towards the great bridge over the River Maas were stalls containing items of clothing such as socks, underpants, handkerchiefs and so on. Further along, more stalls provided sweets and chocolates. At intervals were situated large buckets of red wine and beakers for us to drink from. If any of the Dutch people were seen fraternising with the prisoners, they were made to join the column and forced to walk as far as the German border before being released to make their own way back to Maastricht. The gifts these good people passed on to us were bounty from heaven. As well as the clothing, confectionery and wine, there were toiletries such as razors, soap and flannels. These gifts became our treasured possessions for many months, until in fact we were issued with Red Cross parcels.

Map showing Tom's approximate route on foot from Calais to Aachen after capture in 1940. From Aachen, the PoWs travelled a further 500 miles in a cattle train to Stalag VIII B in Poland.

After crossing the river bridge, our route took us to Aachen in Germany, and after crossing the border the atmosphere changed noticeably with regard to the reception we received from the local inhabitants. From some it was just baleful looks while from others it was downright hatred. There was also the occasional throwing of eggs and rotten tomatoes. We soon came to realise that we were none too popular in those parts.

After many weeks of marching, we finally finished our long hike in the railway marshalling yards at Aachen. After spending the night in the engine sheds, we were entrained onto cattle trucks – twenty-four men to each wagon. We were then shunted back and forth for several hours before finally setting off on a journey into the unknown. We had absolutely no idea of our destination.

Conditions were extremely primitive: just three barred grills to look through on either side of the wagon – that is if one could get near enough to glance out. The journey seemed to go on forever, punctuated only by the occasional stop for the purposes of nature and the issue of some very basic rations – bread and water. Sometimes the train rattled on for hours at a time and then we would be shunted off into sidings to enable troop trains and military supplies to take priority. During one of these long halts, we were informed by a guard that our destination was to be Stalag VIII B near the small village of Lamsdorf (now Lambinowice) in Upper Silesia. This part of southern Poland was a great industrial area, full of coal mines and foundries for the production of steel, etc. After four-and-a-half days on the train, we arrived at a town called Nysa, where we disembarked before being marched several miles to the PoW camp.

CHAPTER 6

NEW HOME

Our first day in the Stalag VIII B consisted of interrogation by interpreters and guards. We were asked for information about our respective units but we had been trained to divulge only our name, rank and number. Our captors seemed quite satisfied with this and did not press too hard. After having our fingerprints taken, our next port of call was the barber's shop. There were several barbers and their job was to shave our heads to the point of baldness. This was to eliminate the risk of body lice. After this we were taken to the

Tom (back row, second left) with his room group in Stalag VIII B. He sent this photograph to Connie, his sweetheart in England.

showers and later to the photographer. At this point we each received a PoW number. The number and photograph were mounted on a small card, which was then stitched onto the right breast pocket of our battledress jacket.

On the afternoon of the second day, we were again paraded before the interpreters and asked what our previous employment had been in civilian life. This was intended to ascertain which type of work we would be most suited to when the time came for us to be sent out on working parties. I had been a lift engineer before joining the army but I did not imagine that I would be employed constructing lifts, so I stated that I had worked on a farm. I thought this would ensure plenty of fresh air and perhaps extra food such as fresh eggs and other farm produce. The Germans, however, had a peculiar sense of humour. Those who had given 'farming' as their occupation were told that it would be the coal mines for them, while some genuine miners from South Wales, Yorkshire, and Nottinghamshire were told that they would be employed on local farms.

Stalag VIII B consisted of a large complex of wooden huts, each designed to house 200 prisoners. There were several huts for stores and a medical block and small hospital. Further away were the toilets, which were very basic. The Guard Room was situated by the main gate and the quarters for the German guards, the administration offices and German officers' quarters were some distance outside the main camp. The camp was also divided into a number of separate blocks in order to house the different nationalities – British, French, Belgian, Dutch and Norwegian. These blocks in turn were subdivided to accommodate army, air force, and naval personnel from each country. The whole complex was surrounded by a 12-foot-high barbed wire fence. Beyond this was 3 feet of 'no man's land' and finally another barbed wire fence 12 feet high. At strategic intervals were eight tall lookout posts, each manned at all times by two guards and equipped with a searchlight at night and a machine gun. Patrolling the perimeter wire there were always two guards accompanied by two German shepherd dogs.

A short distance from our camp, but well within view, was another camp housing Russian PoWs. To all intents and purposes, their camp looked much the same as ours in terms of its general layout. It was in the treatment of prisoners and the issue of rations that the two camps differed greatly. The Russians were not signatories to the Geneva Convention on the treatment of PoWs, unlike the British and Germans. The Germans treated the Russians harshly, and I understand that German PoWs captured by the Russians received even worse treatment from their captors.

An example of these differences is the issue of rations to British prisoners compared to those meted out to the Russians. A kilo loaf of coarse rye bread issued to the British was divided between eight men whereas the same quantity

Above: Russian PoWs at Stalag VIII B were treated much worse than the Western Allies as their nation had not signed the Geneva Convention.

Left: A starving Russian PoW at Stalag VIII B in 1942.

Russian PoWs carry dead comrades at Stalag VIII B, where 1,700 died in one two-week spell alone.

on the Russian side of the wire would be shared between twenty. A dixie of watery fish-head soup was distributed in the same proportions. Unsurprisingly, it was not long before the Russians started dying in great numbers, usually due to dysentery, typhus or hypothermia. Symptoms of typhus included a contagious fever, stupor and delirium. The dead were buried in mass graves and in some cases men were still alive but unconscious when they were thrown into these pits. One ploy used by surviving prisoners was to conceal the bodies of dead comrades for several days in order to draw their rations. Four British army doctors worked in a voluntary capacity in the Russian camp, and it was from them that we obtained news of what was happening there.

Inside each hut in our camp were tables and benches running along one side – two benches to each table and three men to each bench. A gangway ran the full length of each hut and on the other side were three-tier bunks, also stretching the full length of the building. I slept on the top tier of one of these bunks, and this became quite a handicap for me, as I will explain. We were told by an earlier arrival at the camp that if you reported sick at the medical block, you could possibly trade a small article of kit, such as a scarf or balaclava, for cigarettes or tobacco. The exchange would be made with one of the Polish medical orderlies. Another chap and I thought we would give it a go. My story was that I had a large ingrowing toenail; my companion claimed to be suffering from dysentery. Events did not work out as expected, however. The Germans were scared stiff of dysentery and my mate was quickly despatched to the hospital block, there to remain until he was better. I soon wished I had thought of something other than a dodgy toenail. I was told to lie on the table while two German medical orderlies held my feet and a butcher of a doctor prepared to remove my big toenail with what appeared to be a pair of pliers. He put these under the nail and pushed. I very nearly fainted but managed to hold on. I had my foot swathed in bandages for weeks and was supplied with a set of crutches. I persuaded the chap in the bottom bunk to swap with me, but it was six weeks until I was active enough to discard the crutches and walk normally. Once I had made my final visit to have the dressing changed, I kept well away from the medical block. My mate with the alleged dysentery, meanwhile, enjoyed two weeks of relative comfort in the camp hospital and was, I gathered, 'sorry to leave'.

Around two weeks before my departure from the main camp to the coal mine we received a Red Cross parcel issue. It worked out at one parcel between four men. The package was of Canadian origin and included one tin of meatloaf and a large tin of dried milk called Klim. This powdered milk was the best of its kind that I have ever encountered. Other items in the parcel were a packet of tea, a tin of coffee, a small bag of sugar, some prunes, a bar of plain chocolate,

Map showing Tom's PoW travels between 1940 and 1945.

a tin of soup and a bar of soap. Our elation at receiving these parcels was soon tempered when the German authorities emptied the entire contents of each tin into a single container. So we now had a mixture of tea, coffee, soup and so on. The reason given for this flagrant breach of the Geneva Convention was that it ensured the food could not be stored and used in a possible escape attempt. I left VIII B before another issue of Red Cross parcels, so I don't know how this situation was finally resolved.

CHAPTER 7

BELOW GROUND

It was October 1940 when we eventually received orders to proceed to the coal mine, known as Delbruick Shaft and situated between Gliwice and Katowice, not too far from Poland's border with Czechoslovakia. Once again we embarked on cattle trucks for a twenty-four-hour journey from Stalag VIII B to our new destination. The journey was uneventful.

Our new quarters were within the confines of the coal mine grounds but separated from the mining complex by a barbed-wire fence that completely surrounded the prison camp itself. The camp was made up of a row of terraced huts, each self-contained with its own door and accommodation for eight men, including four two-tier bunks, a washbasin, cold-water tap, and in the centre of the room an iron stove. There was also a table and two benches. These conditions were sheer luxury compared to those at Lamsdorf.

We were given two days to settle in and become acclimatised to our new surroundings. The eight men in my hut were of three nationalities – four British, three Australian and one New Zealander. The four British were made up of two Englishmen, one Scot and one Welshman. We all got on very well together. In front of the row of huts was an open space, approximately 20 yards wide and 60 yards long. This was used for the daily roll call and for queuing for the food issue, morning and evening. On the other side of the encampment were the cookhouse and the German quarters for the Camp Commandant and guards. This block also contained the medical room and toilets. Conditions were such a vast improvement on Stalag VIII B that we felt ready to face whatever the future might have in store.

Our introduction to the coal mine came on the third day at 6.30 a.m. After a hasty breakfast of bread, pork fat, and hot mint tea, we assembled for the march over to the pit lift shaft. The majority of the miners were Poles but the overseers were German. Each prisoner was assigned to a particular Pole and we were to remain with him for some considerable time.

Above: Comrades in Harmony, a working party band.

Right: A group of Polish men and women being executed at Hindenburg, Germany, for distributing BBC news items. The picture is among those in Tom's PoW album.

Communication was strictly by sign language at first but we came to understand each other's wishes surprisingly quickly. The level that we were assigned to work at was 1,000 yards (3,000 feet) below ground and over a mile in from the lift shaft. We were conveyed to the coalface by a light diesel engine pulling several small, two-seater trucks. The railway track ran from the lift shaft all the way to the coalface. The shaft was approximately 20 feet across with a height from floor to roof of around 7 feet. We were each supplied with a pit helmet and a miner's lamp. I had imagined that conditions would be so cramped that we would be almost bent double, so I was agreeably surprised to find there was so much room to move about in. The sides and roof of the shaft were re-enforced with pit props and girders situated at a distance of 1 yard from each other.

As the coalface was cut into and the coal and rock extracted, the railway line was immediately extended, as were the shaft's sides and roof reinforcements. Our job was to load the coal wagons that were brought to the coalface in place of the passenger wagons, which were not used again until the end of each shift. The day shift actually commenced at 7 a.m. and finished at 5.30 p.m. We were not given any food to consume during this time and we came to rely on our respective Polish workmate to provide us with a portion of his lunch packet. This invariably consisted of pork fat sandwiches and a flask of ersatz – a coffee substitute. It was good of them to consider us at all, as conditions outside were not much better than those that we experienced.

We soon became accustomed to life below ground, but I must emphasise that having a job to do kept one's mind from thinking too much of home and of how long the war was going to last. We worked on the day shift for thirteen days at a time. On each alternate Sunday we had a rest day and then changed to the night shift. Our Polish colleagues worked to the same timetable so that we remained with them for both day and night shifts.

The food, although meagre, was a great improvement on that at VIII B. We had a loaf of bread and pork fat spread in the early morning before the shift began. This was accompanied by a mug of mint tea. We drank half of this and used the remainder for shaving, as it was a slight improvement on cold water. In the evening we were issued with the same amount of bread and, to go with it, a bowl of swede or fish soup. On Sundays we enjoyed the luxury of soup containing small squares of pork, and on those Sundays when we had a day off, we were given a dessert that usually consisted of jam roll and custard.

The camp guards were nearly all ageing conscripts, some of whom had been PoWs in England or Canada during the First World War. They treated us quite fairly and said that they had been received and dealt with quite reasonably by the British. However, the Camp Commandant was a different kettle of fish. He was known throughout the camp as 'John the Bastard'. It was thought that

Tom (far right) with fellow members of his coal mine working party at Delbruick Shaft.

his parents never married. He really did try and annoy us in any way possible. He would hold roll calls at 4 a.m. or make us wait for our evening meal after coming in from the day shift. One incident I remember very clearly occurred on 26 December 1941. At 4 a.m. the Commandant fired two shots from his revolver into the air and shouted for all to parade 'tout de suite'. He then said, 'I have some good and important news to tell you. Hong Kong has fallen to our gallant allies the Japanese.' Immediately some wag shouted, 'Never mind that. How did the Arsenal get on?' Everyone laughed uproariously and the Commandant looked really sick and deflated. The Germans never did get to appreciate the British sense of humour. Early in 1942 we lost John the Bastard when he was posted to the Russian front and left with our best wishes. I don't think.

As time went on, life became more and more monotonous. Poor food and long hours of work, not knowing how long this situation would last and having to listen to German propaganda day in and day out combined to take their toll and everyone became increasingly depressed and irritable. However, a week or two before our first Christmas in captivity, we had two strokes of good fortune. The first was the arrival of mail from the UK. These letters were the first we had received since setting off for Calais seven months earlier. Since October 1940, we had been issued with one letter-card a month to send to

Tom received this picture of his schoolteacher sister Dorothy with her young charges after he was moved to Stalag 383.

The Stalag 383 stamp appears on the back.

our family and friends at home. Until the first letters from home reached us at Christmas, we had no knowledge as to whether our families had received mail from us or even that they knew we were alive.

After I received my first letter, it was some considerable time before I received any more from home, as in September 1940, during the blitz on London, a bomb completely demolished our house. My mother and youngest sister went to stay with relatives outside London while my father and eldest sister went to live in a flat a short distance from our old address. They had only been there a short time when this block of flats was hit by an incendiary bomb and destroyed. They were both away at work at the time so were unharmed. However, as a result of the two bombings, the family lost everything except the clothes they stood up in. It was many months before I was again able to be in direct contact with members of my family as, of course, my letter-cards were not delivered.

A second stroke of good fortune occurred just in time for our first Christmas as guests of the German Reich. Although we'd had one issue of Red Cross parcels just before we left Lamsdorf, it had taken two or three months for the Red Cross to find us at the Delbruick Shaft. Although we had a slightly bigger food ration than those PoWs who remained in the main camp and were not working, small working parties like ours were not given any priority when it came to the issue of food parcels. Our first delivery of parcels at the coal mine arrived just before Christmas and, although we had to work on Christmas day, we had a right royal feast when our shift finished.

PoWs drink a toast to the Red Cross.

Red Cross parcels came to us from two different sources – England and Canada. After our first issue, the parcels were usually delivered at fortnightly intervals, alternately English and Canadian. One day, whilst opening a Canadian parcel, I found inside a ladies' gold wristwatch that had obviously been dropped by the packer. Through the German authorities and the International Red Cross the owner was eventually traced and the watch returned to its owner in Canada. We learned of this almost eighteen months later, when the Red Cross informed us that the lady in question was both grateful and amazed.

The fortnightly arrival of Red Cross parcels continued until the middle of 1941, when the bombing raids carried out by the Allies had a devastating effect on the German and Polish railways. The result was that the authorities were unable to transport the parcels. To overcome this problem, the Swiss Red Cross later began sending large white lorries – marked with a red cross, manned by two Swiss civilians and loaded with parcels – to all parts of Germany and Poland. They were known to us as the 'White Angels'.

The civilians too had to tighten their belts at this time and our supply of sandwiches from our Polish mining friends dried up. It was as much as they could do to find food for themselves.

On our arrival at the coal mine we were all issued with new battledress jackets and trousers. These were provided by the British government and delivered by the International Red Cross. With the onset of winter, we were each issued with a Polish army greatcoat. These coats were much thicker and warmer than those supplied to the British troops and we soon discovered why this was so. At the beginning of November the snows came and the temperature dropped to several degrees below freezing. Fortunately, each of our living quarters was fitted with a wood-burning stove, situated in the centre of the hut and with a chimney stack going straight up and out of the roof.

On our fortnightly Sunday off, we went out of the camp as a working party to forage for wood to supply the stoves. We did not mind this, as it made a welcome break from the normal routine. Anything that staved off boredom was welcome. In January 1941, however, the snow was several feet deep and dead wood from the nearby forest became even harder to find. We were taken out on these wood-collecting parties by German army transport, accompanied by a spare vehicle to carry the wood. On our return to the camp, we had to unload the lorry and saw the wood into small logs suitable for fuel.

February saw the snow several feet deep on the railway lines and this prevented the movement of coal from the mines to the adjacent industrial areas, thus slowing up production in the steel foundries and other factories. As a consequence of these conditions, all PoWs were ordered to work at snow shifting in order to clear the railway lines. This change of scene was a godsend

Making a hammock from string.

Collecting wood in winter.

to us. We thoroughly enjoyed the romping and snowball fights that ensued. Even the guards received their share of snowballs and some of them actually joined in the fun. We were out all day and had an issue of hot soup and bread at lunchtime.

When we eventually returned to the mine, we were ordered to work in a different section, not this time at the coalface but helping to drive a new shaft through to a previously untouched coal seam. Although we were only labourers on the site and our job was to clear the debris as the tunnel progressed, we soon became quite knowledgeable in the art of tunnelling. This knowledge was later to come in handy in another camp, after our time in the coal mine ceased.

It was amazing what imprints were to be found in the rock face at times – perfect shapes of fossilised fish, all types of shells and patterns of leaves. These were obviously millions of years old and it was amazing to see them so deep below the surface.

We remained on this level of the mine for the duration of our stay at Delbruick Shaft. On entering the mine, our signature tune was 'High hey, high ho, and off to work we go'. The first inkling we had that our working days were numbered came from a surprise visit to our working party by Count Bernadotte. This gentleman was a member of the Swedish royal family and a representative of the International Red Cross. He was the first human contact we had encountered from the Red Cross in nearly two years of captivity. Through him we discovered that NCOs need only work for the Germans in

Hut 303 mine working party in 1942. Tom (back row, second right) sent this picture to his family in Surrey.

a voluntary capacity. This was apparently written in the Geneva Convention relating to the treatment of PoWs. We had never been informed of this by the German authorities, who would have lost a lot of workers had we known. As quite a number of us were NCOs, it was decided by a committee of senior NCOs that we should tell the Camp Commandant that we no longer had a desire to assist the war effort of the German Reich. This caused quite a flap in the higher echelons and was the start of many months of threats of concentration camps and other dire punishments.

During this period of negotiation, we continued to work in the mine and, in our own little ways, slow down the Nazi war machine. This we tried to do in several ways. One popular pastime was to load the coal wagons three-quarters full of bricks and rubble and then top this up with coal. This caused mayhem when the wagons arrived at the surface. Another favourite ploy was to jam the points on the rail track. This would upend a whole train of full coal wagons and cause long delays, as it meant we would have to load the wagons all over again once we had placed them back on the track.

There came a time, though, when things really did seem to get on top of us; there seemed to be a sense of desperation in the air. Chaps were mutilating themselves in order to try and get time off work. One chap put his arm across the railway and allowed a train to run over it. He lost his arm. Another just put his hand on the line and received a few squashed fingers. I too was guilty of joining in the general hysteria. I asked one of my room-mates to pour a pan of boiling water over my right hand. This he did and I could not stop shaking for hours. It was a stupid thing to do, but I had two weeks off work.

The German hierarchy eventually decided we were more bother than we were worth and they would be glad to see the back of us. In January 1943, we were told to pack what few items of personal kit we had and be ready to move out at 6 a.m. the next morning. We had no idea where our next destination would be. For all we knew it might have been a concentration camp. I don't think that anyone seriously believed that this would be our fate, although after hearing later of some of the punishments meted out to other prisoners, I suppose we could consider ourselves lucky.

We had been quite reasonably treated during our two-and-a-half years at the coal mine, although there was one glaring exception to this. This was when two of the chaps managed to escape by cutting through the barbed-wire fence and disappeared into the night. It was a poorly thought-out attempt. For one

A PoW's funeral at the Delbruick Shaft camp.

thing it was winter, and given the weather conditions, it was better being inside the camp than outside it with inadequate clothing, very little food and nowhere to go. Unfortunately, they were soon caught and shot by the Gestapo. Their bodies were brought back to the camp and displayed on the barbed wire for three days as an example to all of us.

Two rather amusing incidents happened to me around this time. Reading material was at a premium in the camp. At one time the only book in circulation was the *Holy Bible*, and the pages of this being very thin, it was soon used up as cigarette papers. One morning I received a parcel from England and it was obvious from its shape that it contained a book. The parcel had been opened by the German officer on censor duties and resealed. Looking forward to a good read, I opened the parcel and removed the contents. The book was *The Evils of Greyhound Racing* by the Revd Dick Shepherd. I make no further comment.

In the second incident, I became one of the few PoWs to have been locked out of a prison camp and refused readmittance when trying to get back in. It happened after another chap and I had forty winks near the end of our shift down the mine and overslept. On waking we found that the shift had finished and all the men had returned to the surface. The PoWs had been marched over to the camp, admitted and then the gates were locked for the night. We, in our turn, walked a mile to the lift shaft and surprised the lift operator by asking to be transported to the surface. We duly arrived at the camp gate and rang the bell. A guard appeared and, using a mixture of English and German, we asked to be let in. He was having none of it. According to him all had been present at the roll call and therefore we would have to remain outside until the morning. We made our way back to the pithead and spent an uncomfortable night, although at least it was under cover. In the morning we were finally allowed back into the camp and, after a quick shower and a hasty breakfast, it was off to work again.

Mining work necessitated a daily shower, something that we were going to miss after our move. Away from the mine, a shower once every two weeks was considered quite sufficient. On that January day in 1943, we were transported to the railway station in army lorries and transferred to a train consisting of one passenger carriage for the German guards and a number of cattle trucks for us. At least we had more room to move than on the two previous journeys. We had not been informed of our final destination and so once again it was a journey into the unknown.

Although conditions were not all that could be desired, it made a nice change from the daily grind that we had just left. We were able to look through the air vents and see that we were leaving the industrial landscape of Upper Silesia and entering an area of forests and farmland. The journey lasted two nights

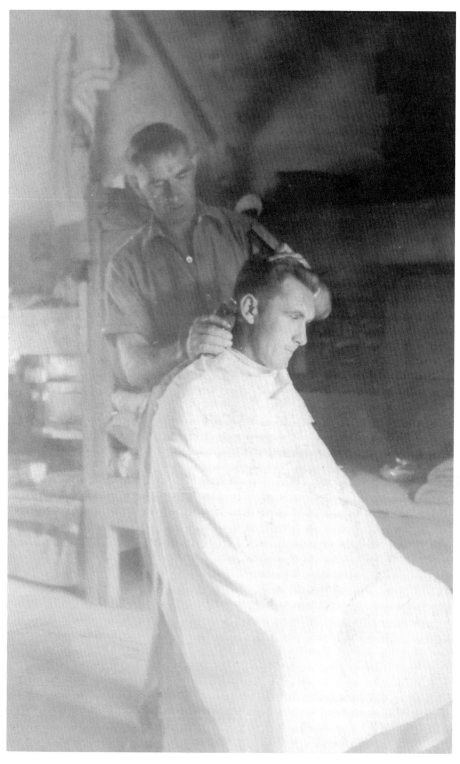

Tom gets a trim.

Stalag 383 at Hohenfels, Bavaria.

and two days, with occasional halts for meals and natural functions. On the evening of the second day we passed through a large city, which we were told later was Munich. We were then told that our final destination was Stalag 383 at Hohenfels, Bavaria. The camp was between Munich and Nuremburg, and we learned later that it was known by the local inhabitants as the 'German Siberia'.

CHAPTER 8

'THE GERMAN SIBERIA'

Our journey to Stalag 383 was completed as it had started, in army lorries, which took us along the snow-clad slopes and through pine forests until we finally reached our destination. My first impression of the camp was the silhouettes of the rather grim-looking watchtowers, the massive double fences of barbed wire, and the ramshackle rows of ice-bound huts with their frosted-up windows. The camp appeared to be situated in a frozen swamp,

The main gate of Stalag 383.

'The camp appeared to be in a frozen swamp miles from anywhere'.

miles from anywhere. You would expect a prison camp to be depressing, but this place exceeded all expectations.

My first night in the place was spent sleeping on the floor of what was known as the 'assembly hut', where all new arrivals went before being allocated permanent accommodation. The cold was one to chill the heart and I settled down for the night clad in my Polish greatcoat, mittens, and balaclava, with two ersatz blankets (made of paper) around me. After a few hours of intermittent sleep, we lined up for roll call, followed by breakfast. This consisted of mint tea and a hunk of brown bread. After this sumptuous repast, we were allocated to our permanent hut accommodation, in my case number 12. This hut was typical of all the 400 in the camp. The asbestos-lined walls were covered with ice; likewise the roof. There were icicles on the hut beams and the solitary window was frosted up on the inside as well as the outside.

We had arrived at this camp when things were at a very low ebb: out of Red Cross parcels, out of cigarettes, out of fuel for the stoves, and out of action generally. These early days were mainly spent lounging about on two-tier bunks, just counting the hours to the next issue of soup. This usually consisted of dried fish heads immersed in boiling water. It was at least hot, and we were grateful for that. There may be more important things in life than food, but not to a prisoner-of-war. Where but in a prison camp would you find a chap flogging his false teeth for a loaf of bread and then borrowing them back to eat it?

A cold winter night at Stalag 383.

The soup queue.

In late February the parcels began to arrive, and for nearly two years we enjoyed the luxury of two parcels a month – one English and one Canadian. Both kinds were excellent and had greatly improved from those issued in the early days of 1940. The Canadian parcel contained a tin of corned beef, a tin of meat-roll, a tin of salmon or sardines, a large packet of sweet biscuits, 2 ounces of cheese, 4 ounces of milk chocolate, a jar of jam, a quarter of tea or coffee, a 1-pound tin of dried milk, and a small bar of soap. The English parcels were less lavish but held an attractive assortment of tinned meats, puddings, and vegetables; a tin of fifty Gold Flake cigarettes, a bar of soap, razor blades and a box of matches.

The arrival of food parcels brought a general lifting of morale and generated a desire among most of us to find ways of passing the time by other means than by just laying about on your bed dreaming of roast dinners and other things that were best left undreamt. When food was short, this was about all anyone could or wanted to do, mainly due to weakness of body and mind. However, as I have mentioned, regular parcels brought strength and energy, and it wasn't too long before we were finding ways of occupying the long days.

We had one large hut in the camp allotted to us for recreational purposes. It soon had several uses, such as a theatre for impromptu concerts, put on some evenings by chaps that had either been on the stage or were connected with the stage in some way. During the day the hut was mainly used as a schoolroom

The weekly handout of Red Cross parcels. 'One day in the week that really mattered,' says Tom's caption in his photo album.

Opening Red Cross parcels. Tom is fourth from left at the back.

A scene from the Camp Theatre Dramatic Club's production of *The Mikado*.

A scene from *The Gondaliers*.

and lecture hall. The leader and instigator of this enterprise was a former schoolmaster and he had a band of willing helpers who formed classes in first aid, languages, Pitman's shorthand, English literature and other subjects. After several weeks, the Swiss Red Cross supplied us with writing materials such as paper, pens and pencils. In time we also received books on first aid from the St John Ambulance Brigade, elementary and advanced textbooks from the Pitman's shorthand publishers, and even books printed in shorthand such as the works of Arthur Conan Doyle.

After some months, the Red Cross was able to arrange for examinations in all our subjects. Successful candidates qualified for Royal Society of Arts certificates. The testing officers for these exams were Germans from the Censorship Office in Munich. My own chosen studies were shorthand and first aid. In the fifteen months that I spent studying these subjects, I was able to take down and read back shorthand at sixty, eighty, and 100 words per minute and eventually received RSA certificates for these speeds. I was also able to read several books by Conan Doyle, written in shorthand. I could practically quote the St John Ambulance First Aid book word for word by the time I took the exam. When the examining officer asked me to define 'shock', I unhesitatingly replied: 'Shock is a sudden depression of the nervous system, occurring after

Scenes from *Up The Pole*.

Above: Serious study.

Right: St John Ambulance Brigade members outside Stalag 383's Ofladium Theatre. Tom (back row, second right) sent this picture to his father in Surrey.

Left: Stalag 383's Medical Officer, Major J. Brooke-Moore.

Below: Christmas 1943 celebrations. Tom is far left at the back.

all forms of accident or sudden illness. The condition may vary from slight faintness to one of complete collapse, where all the vital forces of the body cease to function, and death may result.' All the time I was blurting this out, the officer – slightly shocked at my response, perhaps – was scrambling to find the page. I received my first aid certificate in due course.

Another enterprising activity at Hohenfels was tunnel digging. As a PoW who now had more than two years of mining experience while in Poland, I was roped into the digging squad. I might mention that these tunnels were springing up all over the camp like rabbit warrens. The German authorities were not stupid or blind and they soon twigged what was going on. I believe their thinking was, 'Well, if it keeps them happy, let them get on with it.' When a tunnel was around halfway completed, the guards would mount a sudden raid, 'discover' the tunnel, and supervise while it was completely filled in. We had to be very smart at this game and some tunnels were completed and people made their escape.

Digging a tunnel took a lot of organisation and materials for supplying air to the shaft and material to shore up the roof and sides of the tunnel. The idea was to commence the tunnel from a position immediately beneath the stove that stood in the middle of the hut. Two shovels were acquired from a lorry bringing in a consignment of potatoes and swedes. Props for shoring up the roof and sides of the proposed tunnel were obtained by using each alternate

'Mattie and pals' – and music to break the monotony.

bed board from all eight beds or bunks. The huts were built on stilts so the floor stood at least 2 feet off the ground. The space from the floor to the ground was protected by a double row of weatherboards and, deciding that the bed boards would not be sufficient for the job, we used the inner layer of weatherboards to make up the number. The outer set were still in position so nothing untoward showed outside the hut.

Lighting and ventilation were the two greatest difficulties to overcome. The first of these problems was solved using two carbide lamps obtained from a guard in exchange for cigarettes and chocolate. The ventilation issue was overcome by two home-made sets of bellows, constructed from pieces of bed board and the thick cardboard from Red Cross parcels. After disconnecting the stove chimney and sliding the stove to one side, the work starting the tunnel commenced. The stove stood on bare earth, so we were able to start digging right away. A 2-foot 6-inch square was marked out and the aim was to dig down to a depth of 5 feet before starting the actual tunnel. We all took turns in digging down and others got rid of the dirt by surreptitiously spreading it on the ground. One man was detailed to be on guard to spot the approach of any prowling German guard.

Sawing wood for hut fires. Tom can be seen standing in front of the second hut from the right. As in several other pictures, he identified himself with an X.

'Oxford Circus' in Stalag 383.

At the same time that we were starting our tunnel, a much grander effort was underway in another part of the camp. This rather ambitious tunnel was being dug by some professional miners from Durham and Yorkshire. The digging of their tunnel went on at a much faster rate than ours due to their greater expertise and the position of their tunnel. The overall length of their tunnel was to be 35 yards. This, it was estimated, would bring the escapees out at a point in a small wooded area.

Our tunnel was designed to emerge directly under one of the lookout watchtowers. This left a distance of around 10 yards of open ground to cover before reaching the safety of some trees. This route was chosen because it involved the shortest possible distance. The reason for placing the exit from the tunnel directly beneath the lookout tower was that we could not be picked out by the sweeping searchlight as we emerged. We needed to provide an exit cavity 2 1/2 feet square to allow elbow room for the escapees as they climbed out of the tunnel. A square lid of this size was constructed from the sides of Red Cross packing cases. We intended initially to cover this with grass turfs to disguise the exit.

The digging work was slow going due to the cramped conditions but we made steady progress. We were also unable to remain below ground for long periods. In the meantime preparations were being made for the actual escape.

A lookout tower at Stalag 383. Note the vegetable garden in the foreground.

One or two of the lads had furnished themselves with suits made from blankets by a tailor in the camp. This meant, of course, that they had to sleep without cover at night for some considerable time prior to the escape attempt. Several of us, including myself, felt that it would perhaps be best to travel in simple battledress and carry a pack of provisions for the journey. Our idea was to head for the railway marshalling yards on the outskirts of Munich and from there to board a train heading either for Liechtenstein or Switzerland, both neutral countries in the Second World War.

One morning, when our tunnel was about halfway to completion, we had a surprise visit from a deputation of Gestapo men, all clad in their black raincoats and looking very officious. They came armed with 120 pairs of handcuffs and proceeded to isolate Huts 1 to 15 by placing a barrier between Huts 15 and 16. All PoWs in the first fifteen huts were then handcuffed. The cuffs were linked by a steel chain about 12 inches in length, which allowed a certain amount of freedom for the movement of the hands. The orders were that we remain

'The Chain Gang' – PoWs handcuffed to a chain.

shackled for eight hours a day, for two hours of which we would be handcuffed to the barbed-wire fence. At 6 p.m. each day the guards came into the huts and released us. Apparently, this treatment was in retaliation for a British commando raid on the Channel Islands, when German PoWs were allegedly handcuffed. The chaining to the barbed wire went on for two weeks but we continued to be handcuffed for a further month. After a total of six weeks, we persuaded the guards to leave us the keys to the cuffs so we could release ourselves after they had gone. They agreed to this in exchange for cigarettes. It was not too long after this arrangement that the guards dispensed with the handcuffing altogether. They hung up the cuffs in a corner of each hut with the request that we put them back on if and when any VIPs visited the camp from Berlin. Throughout this time, of course, we were effectively handicapped and unable to proceed with our tunnel digging. I and others were also unable to practise our shorthand, but eventually normal activities resumed (including the digging).

On Sundays we were taken out of the camp to collect wood for the stoves, and we naturally used the breaks from the daily routine to memorise the general layout of the woods through which we hoped one day to make our

PoWs queue to order their copies of *Barbed Wire*, billed as the 'ideal Stalag souvenir'. The picture was taken on the August bank holiday of 1943.

PoWs celebrated the bank holiday with 'one pint per man'.

More bank holiday entertainment.

escape. During one of these forages for wood, I came across an old kettle. Not knowing whether it was serviceable, I took it back to the hut and tested it for leaks. Unfortunately, it would not hold water, but I hit upon an idea to put it to good use anyway. On Saturdays we held camp markets. In the main communal hut, we laid out stalls for the exchange of goods or food. I booked a position on Hut 12's stall and placed my kettle on the bench, covered with a cloth and with a sign beside it saying, 'See the only genuine water otter in captivity. Only one cigarette a look.' I collected around thirty cigarettes that morning.

Work on the tunnel was finally completed in April 1944 and it was decided to make the escape attempt at midnight on 10 April. It was considered unsafe to delay the attempt for too long for fear of the 'goons', as we called the guards, discovering the tunnel. The plan was for one of the helpers to be based at the exit of the tunnel, armed with a torch with which to signal back. One flash for all clear, three flashes for danger. There were eight of us assembled in the hut ready to attempt the break and lower ourselves into the tunnel. I was number five. After number one had progressed some distance into the tunnel, number two was down and ready to proceed when the 'all-clear' was signalled. After number two, the same procedure was adopted by number three and so on.

Quite some time had to elapse between the departures of each escapee, as there was a distance of around 10 yards to dash to the nearest tree cover. This sprint had to be performed when the lookout searchlight was sweeping away from the immediate vicinity. It was emphasised to each escapee that he must not hang around the edge of the wood once he had reached cover. He was advised to move quickly and quietly some way into the copse and then wait for the next man to arrive. As things went, events could not have turned out better. Just as number one prepared to climb out of the tunnel exit, the preliminary air-raid alarm was sounded. This meant that aircraft were approaching although were still some way off. It probably signified a Flying Fortress raid on Munich but for us it meant that the perimeter searchlights were switched off until the all clear was sounded. Thus, we were able to make the escape attempt under complete cover of darkness.

All eight of us managed to make the break into the woods without any alarm being raised. It was around one hour after number one reached cover when I was able to make my dash into the shelter of the trees. There was no sign of the first four so I made my way some distance into the wood and waited hopefully for number six to arrive. The plan was that we would travel in pairs, numbers one and two, three and four and so on. Number one was to wait for the arrival of number two and they would proceed together, not waiting for the others.

The camp was situated between Ausburg and Munich and we estimated that we could reach the railway yards outside Munich in three nights, resting

Stalag 383 at night.

'Something interesting!'

Tom (back row, third left) and comrades in Stalag 383.

up by day where possible. We each had a supply of Red Cross chocolate, raisins and biscuits. The main problem was water. However, we had managed to rustle up four British army water bottles, and these were allotted to each travelling pair. It was decided that it would be advisable to rest up until dawn brought a glimmer of light, sufficient for us to see where we were heading. In any case, we needed the rest after the excitement of the actual escape. The plan was to keep under cover as much as possible and travel on secondary roads, where people and traffic were minimal. Although we could all understand a certain amount of German, which we had picked up from our captors over the previous four years, not one of us was able to speak the language without immediately giving ourselves away. Thus, we had to avoid contact with people at all costs.

This part of Bavaria was mainly forested, so cover was plentiful. When escapee number eight emerged from the tunnel, he replaced the cover to the exit. This was already covered with turfs kept in place by bands of wire from around the Red Cross packing cases. All this was accomplished in the dark, thanks to the US Air Force's bombing raid. It was some three hours before the all-clear sounded, by which time all signs of a breakout had been eliminated by those back in the hut. In the meantime we had all managed to reach the comparative safety of the cover afforded by the trees. It had been decided that we would be safer entering an inhabited area during daylight rather than under cover of darkness, as the latter might arouse suspicion should we be spotted by anyone. Having reached shelter, we settled down to rest for a few hours before making our way to the edge of the wood. It was impossible to sleep, however: the tension and excitement kept the adrenalin flowing. As soon as it was light we made our way in pairs towards the general direction of Munich. Emerging from the cover of the trees, we found ourselves in an agricultural area, with one or two farms visible.

Walking nonchalantly along what we would call a B-class road, we passed several farmworkers. No one took the slightest notice of us. All Germans of military age had long ago left this area, and the people we met were mainly foreign workers pressed into labour battalions by the Third Reich. It soon became obvious to us that these people were too preoccupied with their own thoughts and troubles to take any notice of others. In Germany, in those days, it paid to use discretion and mind your own business.

This part of Bavaria was so removed from the fighting zones that the road direction signs were still in place, so we were able to head directly for the railway yards on the outskirts of Munich. Travelling in pairs, we did not meet up with the other escapees. In fact nothing untoward occurred all day and we estimated that if we rested up for one more night, we could reach our destination by dusk the following day, all being well. We were fortunate that

Domestic chores.

the weather was on our side, and I and my companion found a spot to rest up, in a small copse adjacent to the road. Sheer exhaustion took over and it was daylight again when we came round to face another day.

After a meal of chocolate, raisins, and water, we set off on the road again. It was a repeat of day one. No one seemed interested in us, so we just pressed on – though not too briskly by this time. We had nearly had enough. Almost four years in captivity had taken its toll on our fitness. However, we plodded on, resting for fifteen minutes or so from time to time. Towards evening we came in sight of the railway track and were able to follow it towards Munich. There were lots more people about, but still no one took the slightest notice of us, and we eventually arrived at the head of the railroad. We entered the marshalling yards, where all the goods trains were located. The passenger station was some way further up the line. There were several signs of bomb damage in the area, but all the lines seemed to be intact. There were one or two shunting operations going on. We did not see any of the other escapees and we thought it advisable to get under cover as quickly as possible, as we were conscious of being rather conspicuous.

Much of our planning for the escape was based on information supplied by former escapees. This included directions about routes to follow and the locations of trains destined for Liechtenstein and Switzerland. We intended to

The 'hooch' distillery, which produced wine from fermented raisins.

Stalag 383's Pipe Band in 1943.

follow the same route as previous escapees, who had almost reached Switzerland before they were spotted by German soldiers searching the wagons before the train reached the Swiss border. As a result of this information, we had decided if possible to board a train heading for Liechtenstein. It was not too long a journey and hopefully we would be there before our food and water ran out. We had to be extremely sparing in our consumption of these two commodities.

We soon spotted a train with the word 'Liechtenstein' written on slide-in boards on the side of each wagon. Just as we were about to climb aboard one of these trucks, a face peered out from behind the partially opened door. The face belonged to escapee number two, who hurriedly beckoned to us to join him and his mate inside the wagon. He then informed us that numbers three and four had been spotted entering the railway yards by a German patrol.

Unfortunately, our efforts to escape were quickly extinguished. Some three hours after we boarded the train, it was raided by a posse of German soldiers. Protected by gas masks, they proceeded along the length of the train, spraying a mixture of mustard gas and tear gas into each wagon. Half-blinded, we had no alternative but to surrender. Surprise, surprise: on board the train were fifteen foreign workers as well as we four British army escapees. The civilians were roughly handled and taken away by lorry. We, having displayed the PoW

The thousands of PoWs in Stalag 383 included enough former professional footballers to stage international matches. These are the teams for England v Scotland.

Action from England v Scotland watched by thousands of fellow PoWs.

identity tags that we wore around our necks, were treated quite reasonably, as befits one soldier to another. It would have been a different story had the Gestapo been involved.

We spent the night under guard in an outbuilding in the railway complex. The following day we were transported back to Hoenfels PoW camp by lorry. The journey back took two-and-a-half hours – a good deal less time than it had taken to get there. The outcome of this escapade was ten days in the cooler on two meals a day. These meals consisted of potato soup accompanied by a hunk of black bread and a mug of mint tea.

After our release from detention, we soon settled back into the normal routine of daily life. It was now nearly four years since we were first captured, and we tried not to think of how much longer our captivity would last or whether we would ever get home at all.

Early in June 1944, word filtered through that the Allies had invaded France and the second front had started. This news lifted our spirits no end but seemed to have the opposite effect on our hosts. They became more depressed as the

Goal nets were made from the string used to tie Red Cross parcels.

days went by. We could only gather from this that events were not going their way. From this time on, the relationship between the prisoners and the guards improved no end. This was due mainly to the fact that it had finally sunk into their heads that for them the war was lost. They all became very polite in their dealings with us, and seemed most anxious to co-operate in any way they could.

Unfortunately, the advance of the Allies deeper into Germany and the step-up of bombing by the RAF and US Air Force had one detrimental effect. The bombing of German supply routes and railway marshalling yards caused the supply of Red Cross parcels to slow down and eventually dry up altogether. After four years of deprivation, this was shattering, both physically and

Many PoWs kept rabbits in hutches made from Red Cross packing cases. They were primarily pets but most ended up in the cooking pot or being released through the camp fence.

mentally. After three months without food parcels and only a meagre ration of fish head soup and half-rotten potatoes, our outlook became rather lethargic. It was a matter of survival from day to day – and there were some among us who didn't survive. Our guards were more or less in the same boat. Their rations were cut to a minimum and their previous arrogance became noticeable by its absence. With the food situation as it was, most of the camp's social and sporting activities came to an end and the majority of PoWs took to their bunks for as long periods as possible.

Winter tended to set in early in this part of Bavaria, and by October 1944 the first snows had arrived. It soon became evident why the locals called this part of Germany the 'Bavarian Siberia'. At times the temperature dropped to as low as 23 degrees below zero. Although we had a wood-burning stove in the centre of each hut, we still had icicles hanging from the inside of the solitary window. Most of our time was spent lying on our bunks dressed in all the clothing that we could find – overcoat, socks and so on. There were long periods of boredom punctuated by periods of intense excitement as news of the Allies' advance into Germany filtered through via the one and only radio set left in the camp. This had remained undetected in spite of several unannounced visits by the Gestapo. At the end of one such visit, they were about to leave empty-handed

Stalag 383 funerals. The death rate increased dramatically in the winter of 1944.

A PoW cemetery.

'Coal up!'

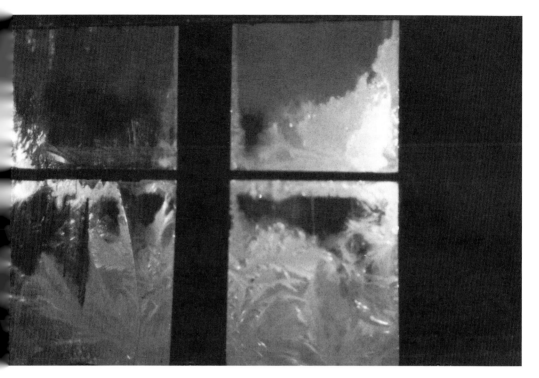

Frost on the inside of the hut window.

Stalag 383 in winter.

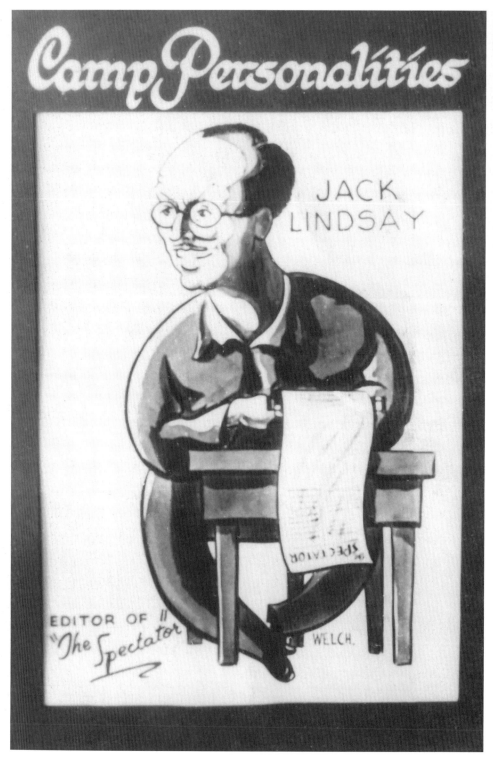

Jack Lindsay, editor of the camp newspaper.

Christmas dinner 1942. Tom is the PoW standing at the back.

Christmas 1943. Tom is second from right at the back.

when they discovered that there was a revolver missing. They then proceeded to turn the meagre contents of each hut upside down. The weapon was never found and they eventually left the camp, having caused as much destruction as they could. You could almost feel sympathy for the poor individual who had lost his revolver. But only almost.

Christmas 1944 arrived. For some of us, it was our fifth Christmas in captivity, and not the best one at that. Early in January 1945, though, we were cheered by the unexpected arrival of two Red Cross lorries from Switzerland. These 'White Angels' were manned by two Swiss nationals – a driver and mate to each lorry. They were all volunteers and were risking their lives, given how much bombing was going on. They had on board enough Canadian parcels for an allocation of half a parcel per man.

CHAPTER 9

LIBERATION

As 1944 gave way to 1945, life proceeded in its now customary humdrum way, although we were occasionally cheered by the latest news of the approach of the Allied forces. The occasional arrival of the White Angels, with half a parcel for each of us, also helped to restore us from the feeble state into which we had slipped during the harsh winter. January, February, and March passed by, and then came April 1945. This was to be the month of liberation. We experienced a hotchpotch of emotions but the predominant one was excitement. Looking back on it, it has taken on all the haziness of a dream.

The Allies crossed the Rhine, and one day early in April, we had news that General Patton's Third Army was moving towards Nuremberg. The Camp

A social evening in 1944.

Discarded Red Cross food tins. In some huts each PoW kept a tin in which to relieve himself on a freezing winter night.

Commandant posted a notice to the effect that there would be no evacuation from the camp. We were to remain in situ until the Yanks arrived to free us. However, within days that order was rescinded. Fresh orders arrived from a higher authority in Berlin that the camp was to be abandoned and all personnel were to be marched towards Hitler's southern redoubt at Berchtesgaden in the Bavarian Alps. This was to be the site of Hitler's mountain retreat. Presumably the intention was to hold us hostage to become Hitler's bargaining counter.

The proposed move came as quite a blow to us, not least because we were hardly fit for a march. However, there was nothing we could do or say that would have made any difference, so we stopped bemoaning our luck and awaited our departure. In any case, there was little time for regret, as we were told that the camp was to be evacuated the next day. We hurriedly packed what few possessions we had accumulated over the years and tried to get some sleep. It was a strange feeling, knowing that this was to be our last night in Stalag 383.

Daylight came, and with it, chaos. The camp went mad. Tables and chairs were smashed up and burnt, and in some cases the sides of the huts were pulled down. The guards were running about like headless chickens, waving their bayonets, shouting and screaming. It was fun while it lasted, and we felt happier

A group of 'Kriegies', as Allied PoWs were known.

'Roll on!'

than we had been for many a long day. We also heard through the grapevine that the Americans had reached Neumarkt, only 30 kilometres from the camp. We were all eventually rounded up and marched out of a ramshackle-looking Stalag. The date was 20 April 1945.

Soon after leaving the camp at 11 a.m., two American Mustang fighter planes passed over dropping leaflets telling the Germans to surrender. The text of the message was 'Why lose your life in the final days of the war?' Those that we picked up were smartly handed to the guards. They seemed quite impressed. Judging by their manner, it was a case of 'the sooner we become PoWs the better'.

Everyone seemed to be heading south, and we soon encountered Poles, Hungarians, and even one or two Russian civilian workers. Some of them had been brought all the way from Budapest for slave labour work. At around 2 p.m. on the first day, we arrived on the banks of the River Regen. As if by mass inspiration, we all sat down, spread along the riverbank and enjoyed a picnic. This consisted of the final remains of our last half of a Red Cross parcel.

The picnic lasted several hours and looked like lasting forever, as if anyone felt less like a long hike than we did, it was the guards. They knew the war was over and shrugged their shoulders with total indifference. We did eventually move, however, and by dusk were around 5 miles from the camp. We rested up in some fields near a Bavarian village. One or two German women came out from their houses with loaves of bread and buckets of water. One who spoke English wanted to know if the American soldiers would harm their children. We assured them that the only people that needed to worry were the SS and the Gestapo, should they fall into American hands.

It was a problem to know what to do – whether to cut a dash for freedom or stay put and wait to be released. However, it was soon decided for us. The same Jerry guards who had sauntered along with us, telling us to take it easy, were suddenly transformed into a bunch of rampant Huns, shouting 'Rouse!' (meaning 'Stir yourselves'), stamping on our brew-up fire and kicking over our tea cans. We soon discovered the reason for this transformation. Another bunch of German guards had come up behind us and it was apparently their duty to take over guard duties from the original camp guards. They were a much more belligerent bunch than our own guards and introduced themselves by firing their rifles into the air, no doubt to warn us that they meant business. If that was the idea, it certainly worked. We smartly packed our few possessions and prepared to continue the march, without argument. From that time on, the march had really started. It wasn't quite the picnic that we had anticipated.

The biggest problem was kit. Most of us were overloaded with blankets and clothing, including greatcoats. Some men had haversacks and water bottles,

Tom (third left, back row) with hut-mates.

and of course we all had whatever food we had managed to salvage, such as potatoes and flour. There was a bright moon that night and there were numerous guards about, so the chances of making a successful break were very slim. One or two must have chanced their arm, though, because during the night several shots rang out. The majority of us reasoned that we had come this far and there was little sense in risking our lives unnecessarily at this stage. Instead we would tread carefully and hope to get home soon.

Next morning we were awakened early and, after a frugal breakfast, we were again on the march. We marched for hours without a break. Our chins were nearly on our knees; we hadn't the energy to talk, so mostly plodded on in silence. Now and then someone would ask a guard, 'How much further?' The reply always came back, 'Noch ein kilo' (Not one kilo), but to us that was a stale old joke that we had heard five years earlier on the march from Calais. The hungry months in camp were now taking their toll and all along the column, men were being forced to dump their packs and blankets. All surplus weight had to go. Every now and then someone would slump to the ground and would have to rely on their mates to help them keep going.

It was around 3 p.m. when we had our first halt of the day. We were marched into a large field cordoned off by water and there were bullrushes everywhere. We surmised that we had landed in a swamp. It made little difference. We were too exhausted to care and went to sleep. Not for long, though. With shouts of 'Rouse! Rouse!' ringing in our ears, we were once again on the move. Our immediate destination was Regensburg, a city in south-west Germany situated at the confluence of the rivers Regen and Danube. The latter, known romantically as the Blue Danube, was a dirty, muddy grey colour and not a bit like I had pictured it in my mind's eye.

Evening came when we were a few miles from the city, and we were allowed to settle down for the night. Most of us enjoyed a fair night's sleep due to sheer exhaustion, but in the morning things looked much brighter. The keen early morning air revived our spirits and we again set off for Regensburg. Apparently our final destination was to be Salzburg, in the mountainous regions, where the Germans planned to have their last stand with PoWs as their final cover. This was approximately 200 kilometres further on, and we had to cross the Danube first. The Americans were not all that far behind us, though. We could actually hear gunfire in the distance. It was a case of, 'Will they reach us before we reach Regensburg?' We finally reached the outskirts of the city on the morning of the fourth day since leaving the camp.

We crossed the only surviving bridge connecting the centre of Regensburg with its outer suburbs. Parts of this beautiful medieval city had been heavily bombed by the Allies, as a result of which large areas had been laid to waste. There were few people to be seen and not a serviceman in sight apart from our guards. We were allowed to remain here for the night. Although we did not know it at the time, this was to be our last night in captivity. When we woke up at dawn, we realised that all the guards had gone. For the first time in five years, we were on our own. It was a strange feeling to be able to wander at will and do as we liked instead of being constantly rounded up and shouted at.

At 10 a.m. we heard the rumble of heavy army transport, and shortly after this a motorised column of GIs arrived on the scene. What a sight for sore eyes! American armoured cars and scout cars swept into the village where we had spent the night. After much handshaking and congratulations all round, we were each issued with two American food parcels. These were known as K-rations and contained two items of food we had not seen for years: fabulous bars of chocolate and tins of beef curry.

This advance party of Yanks did not stay long in the village. They pushed on with their advance deeper into southern Bavaria. They told us they had met only slight opposition during the last few days. The village we were in was almost completely deserted, most of the women and children having left before our arrival. Only a few elderly people remained behind, unable to stand the trauma of evacuation.

The officer in command of the American advance party instructed us to head for Straubing Airfield, where we would be given passage back to the United Kingdom. He said that it would be two weeks before the airport would be able to start evacuating PoWs so we should take our time getting there. 'Meanwhile,' he said, 'enjoy your freedom, try and eat cautiously but enough, and build up your strength.'

Four of us commandeered an old Mercedes Benz banger, and after an initial top-up of fuel from the Americans, we set out on a tour of the area with Straubing our final destination. It was quite an experience. We slept in abandoned houses, even a four-poster bed one night. We arrived at Straubing on the last day of April and joined the waiting list for a flight home.

We had one more dreadfully traumatic experience to endure before we finally left Germany, however. Immediately in front of the plane that was due to take me home was a Dakota carrying twenty-five PoWs. We watched in excitement as it set off down the runway and lifted off, then looked on in horror as it suddenly nose-dived into the ground and burst into flames. Everyone on board was killed. Like myself, some of those on board had been PoWs for five years. All were eagerly looking forward to a reunion with their loved ones. The whole tragedy was too awful to contemplate.

All further flights scheduled for that day were cancelled, and it was two days later when we finally left, also in a Dakota that had obviously seen plenty of action. It looked much the worse for wear and had no bay door. We flew at a very low altitude and finally arrived at Brussels Airport, where we disembarked with a distinct feeling of relief. We were then taken to a local barracks for the night and given plenty to eat and drink. Next morning we boarded a Lancaster bomber for the flight back to England. The pilot and crew gave us all a very warm welcome and a tour of the industrial area of Germany, including Berlin, in order that we could see the bomb damage and devastation. Then it was across the Channel and home to British soil. We landed at Ware in Hertfordshire, and on leaving our plane our first inclination was to kiss the hallowed turf of our homeland. This was a ceremony carried out by all.

We were taken to a camp at Great Missenden in Buckinghamshire and given a shower. It was slightly ironic that this had been a prisoner-of-war camp until recently, housing Italian PoWs. It still had its lookout towers. Someone had a strange sense of humour. After the shower, we had a complete medical check-up and an issue of clothing, including battledress. It was 13 May 1945 – five years less thirteen days since the date of my capture. We were also given travel vouchers and ration cards before finally leaving for our respective homes.

Tom in 1945.

Tom and Connie on their wedding day.

There was no counselling in those days. My previous home in East Dulwich, London, had been flattened by a German bomb, so I went to my family's new home at Coulsdon, Surrey.

I was given a grand welcome, but it took several months before I settled down and adjusted to civilian life again. I never really found tranquillity until I returned to Dorset to be reunited with Connie, the girl I had met on the tennis court at Charlton Marshall in 1940. We became engaged in August 1945 and married in April 1946. We have no regrets. We were in love then, and still are. April 1996 will be our golden wedding anniversary. God willing.

Thomas Reginald Guttridge,
October 1995

POSTSCRIPT

BY ROGER GUTTRIDGE

Although my father eventually made a full recovery from the traumas and deprivations of war and captivity and went on to live a long and active life, his experiences undoubtedly and inevitably took a toll in various ways. My mother often told me that in the early years of their marriage, Dad had recurring nightmares during which he relived his war experiences, even using pillows to build barricades in his sleep. But I also had the impression that witnessing some of the horrors of war gave him a more philosophical outlook when dealing with the occasional horrors of everyday life.

Following their marriage, my parents lived initially at Coulsdon, Surrey, not far from Dad's family. My father initially returned to his brief Civvy Street role as a lift engineer while my mother became an office worker at County Hall, London, headquarters of what was then the London County Council. I was born in May 1950 and seven months later we moved to my mother's native county of Dorset, where my father began a new career as a telephone engineer. After retirement in 1974, he revisited his military roots to spend five years as a storeman at Blandford Army Camp.

Throughout these years my parents lived in the small town of Sturminster Newton and the nearby hamlet of Fiddleford, just 12 or 13 miles from Charlton Marshall, where they had met in 1940. My only brother, Philip, was born in 1954 but suffered brain damage at birth and died three months later.

My parents did indeed live to celebrate the golden wedding that my father refers to in the last line of his manuscript. Both remained active for some years after that. Dad was known for his helpfulness to others and especially for his sense of humour and practical jokes, and was a popular member of his adopted community. Just how popular became evident after his death in March 2004, when several hundred people turned out for the funeral of a man who, at the age of ninety, had outlived most of his own generation. It was a remarkable tribute. My mother died in 2013, aged ninety-one, having fulfilled her ambition to 'live longer than Tom'!

Unlike some former servicemen I have met, my father was always happy to describe his war experiences to anyone who expressed an interest. Occasionally he would also bring out the album of photographs of Calais and the PoW camps, which he had brought back from the war. I believe he obtained these pictures by trading cigarettes and other items from Red Cross parcels. In May 1965, I travelled with my parents to Calais for a ceremony commemorating the twenty-fifth anniversary of the battle.

In the early 1990s, when newspapers were busy publishing supplements marking the fiftieth anniversaries of various Second World War events, I wrote many features and interviewed veterans, evacuees, and others about their experiences. My father was among them. This in turn prompted me to suggest that he write down all his war memories and that, combined with his collection of photographs, they would make an interesting book. The plan was that I would help him to get them published. By this time I was a freelance journalist and author and, being busy with my own projects and preoccupied with making a living, it was something that I 'never got around to'. Dad made it clear that he was not happy with me over this and eventually had

Tom (right) with his old Rifle Brigade pal Charles Poultney at Green Jacket Close, Winchester.

some photocopies made of the manuscript, added covers and bindings, and distributed them among family and friends.

I redeemed myself to some extent by serialising extracts in a local newspaper and by reuniting him with old comrades. These included his Rifle Brigade chum Charlie Poultney, whom we visited at his home in Green Jacket Close, the regiment's retirement accommodation at Winchester, and Reg Willbourne, of Southampton, who was in the King's Royal Rifles and was also captured at Calais, became a prisoner-of-war in Poland and worked down the mine. Using materials that included a water bottle, a crystal obtained from an elderly woman in the camp kitchen and headphones acquired from a Polish dentist who treated him for toothache, Reg constructed a radio that kept fellow PoWs informed of war developments and became a great morale booster. The aerial was a length of copper tape smuggled out of the camp's electrical workshop and the device was powered by plugging an adaptor into an electric light socket. The cleverest feature of all was a tube inserted into the water bottle and filled with water. 'I left the bottle hanging on the door. Jerry knew we had a radio somewhere but

Tom (right) with fellow former Stalag VIII B PoW Harry Malpass.

whenever they picked up the bottle, they saw the cork and water and put it back,' Reg told my father and me when we visited him at the Royal South Hants Hospital in February 1993. The unique wireless not only survived the war but returned with its creator and is now in the Royal Green Jackets Museum at Winchester.

Our hospital meeting with Reg was an especially moving occasion because not only were these two old comrades able to share war memories but Reg also told us he was dying of cancer and had come to terms with his imminent passing. He died just twenty-one hours after our visit and I published his story in the *Southern Daily Echo* the following week.

Others who contacted us included another former PoW, Harry Malpas, of West Moors, Dorset, who said reading Dad's memories in the newspaper was like 'reading my own life story'. Harry was wounded and captured at Dunkirk in 1940 and spent four-and-a-half years in Stalag VIII B, where he too worked down a mine. Tom and Harry could not recall meeting in those days but spent three happy hours reliving their memories.

In 2013, more than a decade after the last of these meetings, something wholly unexpected occurred to give me new impetus in getting my father's book into print. As part of my research for a book of a very different kind, I joined an audience of around sixty people at a non-religious demonstration of mediumship near my home in Dorset. This was soon after my mother's death and, after passing on some information from her, the medium, Micky Havelock, told me and the rest of her audience that my father was 'muscling in' on the communication.

'He's showing me books wall to wall,' she said.

I had met Micky once before at a similar event but she had never been anywhere near my home, which made her comment all the more convincing. It was not the first time I had received such specific information, but that's another story.

'That's my house,' I said. 'I have 10,000 books at home. They literally are wall to wall.'

'I need to be careful how I say this because I know you've written books yourself,' she said. 'But I'm seeing a book with your father's name on it. He feels he should have his name on the cover of a book.'

'I think I know what that's about,' I said. 'He wrote a book featuring his war memories and I was supposed to get it published for him but I never got around to it.'

'It was left for you to do and you haven't done it,' said Micky, to the audience's great amusement. 'So get on with it!'

Four years later, I have 'got on with it'. Finally, posthumously, my father has his name on the cover of a book.

ACKNOWLEDGEMENTS

On behalf of my late father as well as myself, I am grateful to all who have contributed to this book, including my son Andrew Guttridge for inputting his grandfather's manuscript some years ago; my wife Sylvie for preparing the two maps and scanning 100 photographs; Mark Churchill for his help in identifying the house at Charlton Marshall where Dad was billeted in 1940 and Mr and Mrs Robert Harman for allowing me to photograph it; Barry Cuff for the two Blandford photographs; staff at the Royal Green Jackets Museum, the Hampshire County Archives and the Oxfordshire History Centre for information on and historic pictures of Winchester Barracks; and to all those comrades, fellow PoWs, Red Cross volunteers, and others who helped my father to survive the five most challenging years of his long life. And to Dad himself for leaving me such an interesting collection of memories and photographs.

Roger Guttridge